W9-BER-416

Temple B'nai Israel
The History of a BOI

Jimmy Kessler

2004
136th Anniversary of B'nai Israel
Galveston Island, Texas

NORTEX PRESS  Austin, Texas

For the Members of
B'nai Israel
Past, Present, and Future
and
Shelley, my BOI

FIRST EDITION
Copyright © 2004
By Jimmy Kessler
Manufactured in the U.S.A.
By Nortex Press
A Division of Sunbelt Media, Inc.
Austin, Texas
ALL RIGHTS RESERVED.
1-57168-987-7

Contents

Preface

B'nai Israel is a statement. It is a statement of commitment by Jews to the preservation of their religious heritage. A founding member of the Reform Jewish movement in America, it has been a significant presence within its community. Its history reflects the entrepreneurial talents of its members, the tenacity of its Rabbis and it's impacting presence in Galveston.

B'nai Israel is a BOI. The letters BOI (born on the island) have been an acronym for those individuals who trace their roots to Galveston Island, a true island located in the Gulf of Mexico, just off the coast of Texas. More than a label of nativity, it represents a descriptive eponym that conveys uniqueness. More so, it conveys a pride of specialness that even rivals being a Texan. When the bridge that connected Galveston to the mainland had a draw span in its middle, it was said that all things of importance stopped at that span - the Island side, that is. For the true B.O.I., once one traveled to the Galveston side of that span all that really matter was

Galveston thought and life and the rest of the world be damned.

B'nai Israel is as proud and independent as is the island it calls home. This dignified congregation is representative of the American Jewish community and has been so for 136+ years. The following pages are part of its history.

Introduction

This volume is essentially the text of the doctoral dissertation I submitted to the Hebrew Union College—Jewish Institute of Religion in June 1988. At that time, the arbitrarily selected ending date of the data was 1976. More over, it is based on the recorded minutes of the Temple's Board of Trustees.

In celebration of the one hundred and thirty sixth year of Temple B'nai Israel, this publication has a data ending date of 2003.

The preparation of this history involved more than just this writer.

Grateful thanks to the Virginia Messer, Amber Stanfield, and the staff at Eakin Press who were of most helpful assistance.

The publication of this volume was in no small part made possible by the H. Kempner Family. Their support of B'nai Israel, since 1874, has clearly allowed for a significant part of this history to have occurred, let alone recorded.

Robert Goldhirsh, president of Temple B'nai Israel, Nat Shapiro, first vice-president of Temple B'nai Israel and Dr. Marshall Stein, treasurer of Temple B'nai Israel, and Mrs. Lynn Levin Cantini were of incredible support in bringing this book into print.

The Temple's secretary, Vicki Diaz, was of boundless assistance in assembling the material needed to update this volume.

The ever available expertise of Steve Nussenblatt allowed for the presentation of the photos in this book.

From the rich resources of Temple B'nai Israel, came a most special member and secretary of the Congregation to provide editing services. The assistance of Dr. Carla Wills Brandon, a well-known published author, was price-less.

A most special thanks to Shelley Kessler, my bride and life partner, for her effort in the writing of the dissertation and this volume. She was the first and ultimately, the last commentator. Without the blessing of her presence, neither work would have come into being.

Most of all, deep appreciation to the members of Temple B'nai Israel to whom this book is dedicated from whom this history springs eternal.

Obviously the author accepts responsibility for the contents of the work.

The Origins of B'nai Israel

Most likely the first Jewish services in Galveston were held in the home of Isadore Dyer during the High Holydays of 1856. Unfortunately, there are no records that attest to this event. The earliest documented services appear in extant records found in the October 8, 1859, edition of the Weekly News. This reads as follows:

"DAY OF ATONEMENT. Today being the 10th day of the Jewish 7th month 'Tishri,' our Jewish fellow citizens have closed their places of business to celebrate it as a day of fast and prayer, according to Leviticus, Chapter 25, commencing verse 27."

The first mention outside Temple records to form a congregation is the short statement found in the Weekly News dated July 26, 1868, "VARIOUS ITEMS. The Israelites give notice of a meeting today, to organize a reform congregation."

Based on verbal lore, its assumed that some form of services were going on in Galveston before 1856. If this Jewish community was in any way historically similar to others in the United States, the first Jewish settlers had to arrange for burials and the observance of the Jewish High Holy Days. Along with this, there would be a strong need to establish a house of worship.

The earliest Temple record can be found in the oldest bound minutes book and are dated August 16, 1868. This entry indicates that there was a "general assembly" meeting that produced resolutions to be acted upon by an Executive Committee. It appears that the initiators of that first meeting even consulted with a local judge, E.T.Austin about the organization papers necessary for the incorporation of the Congregation. As was characteristic at that time for the establishment of a synagogue, a Mr.Blum suggested that the Executive Committee send letters "abroad to solicit funds for the establishment of the congregation." In addition, the Executive Committee voted to require a $10,000 bond for the Treasurer and a $2,000 bond for the Secretary. Moreover, it was voted that the Secretary could only maintain $100 in monies turned in for payment.

The first meeting of the Executive Committee that preceded the first general assembly took place in the office of S.K.Labatt. At that meeting it was decided the Executive Committee would have regular monthly meetings for the daily running of the Temple. The first officers of the Congregation were I.W.Frank, President, S.E.Loeb, Vice President, S.K.Labatt, Secretary, and M.Kopperl, Treasurer. At that same August meeting, D.Wenar and S.E.Loeb were asked to organize the first High Holyday services for the coming year.

On September 6, 1868, it was reported that Judge Austin provided the incorporation papers without charge. Then on October 10, 1868, the Executive Board voted to purchase a suitable lot for the building of a synagogue. The funds to pay for the building were to come from subscriptions that would be sought from locals as well as from those in other cities. These pledges would be collected by solicitors appointed by the Executive Committee. The President then appointed I.Dyer, I.C.Levy, M.Kopperl, S.C.Loeb, and Cohen to select a site for the Temple in the "central part of the city."

In reviewing these early records its clear that even though all the necessary, perfunctory activities to begin a congregation were of major concern of this early group, there was still room for the human side of life to be recorded. At the November 8, 1868, meeting, it was decided that if one was late for meetings, they would be fined $2.00. Even Executive Board members could be fined. At the December meeting of that year, the Secretary was reminded to be more diligent in his duties and was then fined $2.00 for being late.

By 1869, Congregation B'nai Israel was well on its way to its position of prestige in the growing port city. On April 18, $5,360 had been pledged for the building and land, and $2,708 of those funds had been collected. Among these early subscribers were I.Dyer, L.Oppenheimer, Wenar, Dinklaker, Flatto and Levy, Rosenbaum, Reinauer, H.James, A.M.Gusik, Bass Hutchins, G.Willig, T.W.M.Mahan, M.Kopperl, S.K.Labatt, Greenlease Block and Co., A.Sepums and Co., Ranger and Co., Arnold and Bros., L.Block, B.Tierman, A.Flake, Finberg, Kory, Wenly and Co., Sonnentheil and A.Block. Due to the funds collected and pledged, the Executive Committee authorized the Treasurer to purchase "City Company scrip" to pay for two lots in the downtown city area. $4,275.00 was used for the purchase of this land.

June 13, 1869 saw the recording of the following additional gifts for the building:Richards and Hawkins, Jalonick and Smith, L.Kauffman and Co., Max Maas, W.Lockuse, N.Pastermann, M.Strickland, A.W.Weiss, Watson and Vistor, Julius Levy, T.B.Stubbs, J.Sautess, Corn Ermis, T.D.Douglas, I.Bernstein, S.Heidenheimer, I.W.Frank, B.R.Davis and Bros., I.Fedder, Mc Galpain, I.H.McCormick, Brown and Sang, Amiler and Mason, R.F.George, I.B.Root, L.Klopman, W.H.Sellers, D.D.J.Robira and E.S.Jamison.

In reviewing the names of the early Jews on the Island and the names of the contributors, it is clear that the non-Jewish community provided a respectable portion of the subscribed funds. In order to accomplish the building of the new Temple, a plan was adopted on October 10, 1869 to sell $20,000 worth of bonds. The subscribers would pay them out and they would earn 8 percent interest redeemable either at the end of twenty years or at the discretion of the Temple. Those who participated and were members, would be given the option to buy pews with life rights (except in some circumstances that were not clearly identified). In December, 1869, a ball was organized to raise money for the building of the Temple. There were committees for invitation delivery (I.Kahn), for the rental of a hall, for the printing, for the music, and for the entertainment. In the January minutes of the Temple Board meeting, it was reported that a profit of $901.23 was made from the Ball, but that they also spent $73.00 on wine.

From the beginning, the congregation seemd to be in alignment with the Reform movement, though nowhere in the early minutes is such a decision found. Because Galveston was still a frontier settlement, it is likely Reform was selected as it best fit the needs of the congregants at that time. Reform provided them with a way to maintain a tie to a synagogue without demanding ritual observances. Rigid observance would be beyond their abilities on "Snake Island." Moreover, the ethical and religious teachings of early Reform permitted the Jews of Galveston to find a comfortable place in the community.

The year 1870 was most monumental in the history of the Temple. During that year, Temple B'nai Israel officially opened the doors of its building. On March 27, 1870, the minutes reflect that S.K.Labatt was asked to secure a charter for Congregation from the next session of the Texas Legislature.

Though it is believed that Temple B'nai Israel is the oldest congregation in Texas, it's not the holder of the oldest state charter. Temple Beth Israel of Houston holds that distinction even though Houston was not as old a city as Galveston. Some of those charter members in Houston had originally come from Galveston. However, no explanation is given for the delay in requesting a charter from the State.

In April, 1870 the plans for a building were presented by Mr.Stewart and a cost of $9,200.00 was quoted for the completed structure. In 1890, Nicholas Clayton would design an addition to the building structure that would create the unique design by which the Temple would be known.

The original contract for the Temple called for the brick work to be done by Mr.Prichard and the wood by Scott and Gilman. The architect agreed upon was Mr.Stewart. A committee of Dyer, Kahn, Heidenheimer, Kopperl and Frank were appointed to oversee the building of the structure. During this same time, a committee of Kory, Kahn and Fedder were asked to sell bonds at 10 percent interest per year with ten year maturity. This would be used to finance the "brick building".

With a June 9, 1870, date set, the Executive Committee of the Temple invited Mr.Tuck, the Grand Master of the Masonic Lodge of Texas, to lay the cornerstone. In addition, Mr.Jacobs, Rabbi of the New Orleans Portuguese Synagogue, was invited to officiate at the ceremony. It is a traditional belief that this was the first time an ordained Rabbi functioned in Texas. Mr.S.E.Loeb served as the Marshall of the affair.

The first mention in Temple records of the Hebrew Benevolent Society, that pre-dates the Congregation, appears here. The records show that the organization was invited to participate in the cornerstone placing. Mr.A.Allen donated the cornerstone of the building.

At the July 3, 1870, meeting of the Executive Committee, it was reported that the Temple was $5,000 short of the cost of the building. Mr.M.Felix Wolf was authorized to solicit funds to make up this deficit in the New York City area. At the July 31st meeting, it was reported that I.Dyer and F.Messinan, executors of Rosanna Ostermann's estate, were ready to transfer to the Temple $5,000 that had been left in her will for the building of a synagogue.

August 14, 1870, a report was made for the building of galleries in the sanctuary because the Temple needed more room to accommodate the growing congregation. During the same meeting the charter of the Temple was delivered, and the check for $5,000 was presented by the Ostermann estate. In June of 1870, Mrs.Bennett and Mrs.Hinkle gave the Temple "a copper box to put in the stove to receive such articles as was to be deposited." During that same year, the Congregation lost several members including the entire family of Joseph Lyons, Joseph Henry and Charles Blum. The sinking of the Varuna, one of the many small ships plying the Gulf Coast, claimed the lives of these early congregants. The minutes for November 6, 1870 reflect these deaths.

By 1871, Congregation B'nai Israel was functioning in almost all aspects, just as if it were a long established Temple. In February of 1870, the Constitution had been amended to establish four General Assembly meetings for the entire Congregation in November, February, May and August of each year. The first General Assembly on February 17, 1871, called upon the membership to attend an auction for pews. The pews would start at a minimum price, but were expected to bring in higher amounts. At this "public question," the life pews of those in arrears would be available as well as unsold ones. The pew tax was then $6.00 per year. In addition, it was ruled by the congregation that any person who leaves the membership of the Temple, loses the rights to his family pew.

The first pew list of the Temple dated February 27, 1871, included the following with their name, pew and seats:Joe Levy 3:1,2; M.Schram 3:3,4,5; I.Fedder 3:6,7,8; I.A.Levy 5:1,2,3; D.Freeman 9:3; Sylvan Lyon 21:1,2,3 and 23:1,2,3; I.Bernstein 31:1,2,3; I.Rosenfield 40:1,2,3; I.W.Frank 47:2,2; I.Heyman 50:1; S.I.Levy 55:1,2,3; L.Block 50:1,2,3; F.Halft 61:1,2,3; M.Marx

65:1,2,3; A.Cohen 72:2,3; I.Finberg 12:1,2,3; M.Arnold 15:1,2,3; M.Rosenbaum 17:1; H.Loeb 17:2,3; D.Wenar 14:1,2,3; M.Schwartz 24:1,2,3; L.C.Michael 32:1,2,3; I.Holstein 39:1,2,3; G.Lewis 42:1,2,3; A.Weiss 48:2,3; H.James 50:2,3; I.Feist 57:1,2,3; A.Dreyfus 59:1,2,3; L.Blum 63:1,2,3; and Sylvan Levy 73:1,2,3. If everyone paid the price explained in the chapter on finances, the first sale would have produced $14,012.50 for the Temple.

On April 9, 1871, the Young Men of Galveston, a local social club, gave $310.00 toward gas fixtures for the Temple. At that time, the membership of that organization included A.Blum, I.Blum, E.Kauffman, B.Blum, A.Weil, A.Ortlieb, I.Davis, H.Vogel, I.Wenk, A.Levy, R.Carrow, S.Block, I.Gottshalk, G.Levy, M.Block, A.Koenigsberger, E.Cahn, I.Lovenberg, B.Levy, S.Kauffman, M.Block, I.Schornstein, L.Weiss, R.Weiss, M.Rosenbaum, L.Migel, R.T.Morris, L.Lewis, G.Mayhalft, S.Mayer, I.Sonnentheil, M.Levy, and E.F.Weill.

At that same period, Mr.Lyon offered to "sell" the Temple a "sefor" for $100.00. The minutes do not record if the Temple accepted the offer or if this was a Torah scroll read in the Temple during services.

In May of 1871, the Temple made a major step in building its longstanding reputation for having outstanding musical accompaniment to its services. By purchasing its first organ from Goggan Brothers for $325.00 Temple B'nai

Israel's musical foundation was laid. At the same May 21st meeting, it was moved and seconded to suspend the rules and allow members to take off their coats during the meeting on because of the Island heat. That motion lost with 8 voting for and 11 against. It was then moved and seconded to adjourn. 15 voting for and 15 against adjournment. There being a tie, the President decided not to adjourn. It was then again moved and seconded to adjourn. This time it carried." With this particular meeting, if one type of heat did not overwhelm the members, clearly another sort must have done so.

During the first fifteen years of Temple B'nai Israel 's history, one of the major concern was the building of the Temple's first structure and the securing of the funds to accomplish this task. The Hebrew Benevolent Society, a burial society that is the oldest Jewish entity in Texas, had already been in existence and had established the first cemetery in 1852. Knowing this history, it is fair to surmise that the Temple did not have to be preoccupied with creating a cemetery. The motivation for a congregation and a structure was the community's desire to be like their neighbors who had already established local churches. By their actions these early frontier Jews not only became more American, but more Texan.

The Temple at Work

As the Temple enters the 1870's, it becomes clear from the minutes that its continued development was an ongoing enterprise. B'nai Israel began to rapidly experience the normal activities of a congregation. A significant amount of effort brought the Temple into involvement with the larger Jewish community in the United States. On August 24, 1873, a circular was received from a new group calling itself the Union of American Hebrew Congregations. A later notice dated June, 1874 informed congregations across the United States of a meeting in Cleveland, Ohio in July of that year. The Board of Congregation B'nai Israel appointed Mr.Halff as their delegate because he was going to be in Cleveland at that time. On June 20, 1875, the Congregation voted to become a charter member of the U.A.H.C. Mr.Kopperl, Halff and Rev.Blum were appointed as delegates for the next meeting of the Union on June 13, 1876, in Buffalo, N.Y. In spite of the far travel to meetings, this small group saw to it that in 1877 M.Kopperl and

L.Oppenheimer were authorized delegates. In 1879, L.Oppenheimer represented Congregation B'nai Israel. To this day, the Temple has continued their U.A.H.C. membership.

In 1892, Leo N.Levi suggested that the Temple adopt the new prayerbook of the Central Conference of American Rabbis, called the Union Prayerbook. This step further reflects the clear path selected by the membership of the Temple in their identification as American Reform Jews.

From its inception, the choir was a significant part of the fabric of the Temple. In July 1879, Rev.Mr.Blum, the rabbi, was given complete control over the choir. Though the choir was primarily voluntary, there were always paid members

The rabbi of the Temple was responsible for the choir, along with an appointed member of the congregation, or a committee was appointed to be directly involved with the choir. The first choir manager was Mr.L.Schlesinger. He was appointed by the Executive Committee on March 7, 1886. Up until then, Mr.A.Frankel did much work with the choir. In recognition of his active envolvement, he was given a testimonial on February 18, 1886, for $220.00. As early as November 16, 1885, the Temple was paying over $600.00 per year for the choir and the very next year, the cost went up to $900.00. On March 27, 1905, it was recorded that the choirmaster was paid $30.00 per month and the choir voices cost $85.00 per month. By the 1970's, the Temple was spending over $7,000.00 for its regular weekly choir and over $3,000.00 more for voices on holidays and special services.

For several decades pews became a continuing issue of concern. On May 2, 1875, the minutes record that locks were authorized for pews to keep strangers from taking unauthorized seats at services. It would be appropriate to assume that originally there was some sort of low door or gate, that could be locked. This would have been done to prevent entry to the aisle of the individual pews. On May 30th, that permission was rescinded. On October 31, 1875, the Temple was sued by one member for a pew that was in the hands of another member. Pews indeed were a very big issue.

The edifice of Temple B'nai Israel was a symbol of a permanent Jewish presence. Just as the major religious movements kept their houses of worship in good repair, so, too, did the Jewish community. In October of 1886, Nicholas J.Clayton, an architect was consulted on enlarging the Temple. Leo N.Levi was appointed chairman of a committee responsible for overseeing this new project. In March, 1887 the front wall of the building began falling away and the Temple was deemed unsafe. By May, 1887 another committee consisting of Leon Blum, H.Kempner and Leo N.Levi had been appointed to deal with the needed additional building repairs. By that date $6,100 had been raised for the expenses. Through the good offices of President Mrs.J.Sonnenthiel, the Ladies Benevolent Society loaned the Temple $500 toward the repairs. In January, 1888, forty-two incandescent lights were ordered for the Congregation at a cost of $10 per month. Eleven months later it was noted that the Temple heating system was going bad and would need replacing. On May 18, 1890, the Temple Board received a bid from Nicholas J.Clayton, Architect, for $12,000.00 to remodel the building. Two months later, the Board accepted the bid of Harry Devlin for $6,225.00. Harry Devlin would carry out Clayton's plan to remodel and enlarge the original building.

In 1890, the Board decided to purchase a new organ from Geo.Jardine and Son. The presence of an organ as well as a choir was always important to the life of the Temple. This particular instrument was unique in that it was water powered. Unfortunately the City of Galveston refused to allow a water powered motor. Because of this another system had to be found. At first an electric motor was suggested, but Galveston did not have such a system. In addition, such a motor, typically an Edison motor system, was not considered reliable. Hence,they went to a hand operated bellows.

Even though Galveston had electricity in 1883, the Temple could not make use of it until 1896. At that time two bids were received to electrify the building. D.L.Goble and Co.submitted a bid for $314.60 for 94 bulbs, but it was the Barden-Sheets' bid of $165.00 for 105 lights that was approved. The following year the trolley lines were available to deliver electrical service, so the organ was converted to electrical power.

In 1906 there were even more improvements to the Temple. The Board voted that only full length memorial windows in the Temple would be allowed. They agreed to accept the Ladies Auxiliary's offer to pay for the raising of the sidewalk around the Temple. By 1907 181 members belonged to the Temple. In that year, a new Torah was donated by the Albert Aron family. Along with this, stained glass windows were installed by the families of, and in memory of, Max Maas, Mrs.M.Schram, Mrs.Leon Blum and Sam Migel.

Over the century plus of the Temple's life, many gave of their strength to add to hers. Among those families who often stepped forward with giving fervor, were the Kempners. In June of 1916, Mrs.Eliza Kempner agreed to put up a Community House, as long as the cost did not exceed $7,000, and if other repairs were done to the Temple. The following year, Mrs.Kempner provided for the Sunday School with the Kempner Memorial Hall. This most generous gift was accepted at a gathering of the Temple, the International Order of B'nai B'rithand the Temple Society. In 1922, the Kempner family again stepped forward and purchased a new organ at a cost of $12,000.00. In that same year, the Congregation was able to afford a new heating system at a cost of $8,775.00, a new basement floor and a new roof.

In 1924 a board was created to build a Community House offered by Mrs. Kempner in 1916. By January 29, 1928, it was decided that the name of the facility would be the Henry Cohen Community House, and the cost for this project was set at $80,000.00. The funds were raised with a substantially larger amount than their original pledge being contributed by the Kempners.

On May 17, 1948, a proposal was made to build a new Temple at a cost of $225,000.00. The Board also adopted a proposal noting the cost of $10,000.00 just to move the organ and another 5 percent cost for the architect. On July 21, 1948, a special meeting was held to approve the building of the new facility. Land was then purchased on 35th and L on November 8, 1948 at a cost of $15,500.00. The Temple had a hard time raising the necessary funds to build the new building. In 1951, Dave Nathan announced that the Kempner family would give $60,000.00 in honor of their mother, if the Temple would raise a matching $90,000.00 in thirty days. When this was not done, the Kempners extended the deadline for another 60 days. Even though the matching gunds were short by $4,500, on January 7, 1952, the Board authorized the building with the Kempners giving $75,000.00. The location was changed to 30th and O and the land was then purchased for $40,000.00. In

September of 1952, a special meeting was held to view the building plans. During this meeting, the Masonic Lodge offered $80,000.00 for the original Temple and Community House. The offered was accepted. The total cost of the new Temple would be $271,355 for the building, $19,900 for the electrical work, $5,840 for the plumbing, $46,993 for the air-conditioning, $6,300 for the pews, $2,000 for the landscaping, $38,000 for the land and $15,000 for the architects.

Among the many entries in the minutes are those which concern the general community welfare. Each, individual account, or minutes, tells a story. Each account expresses the concern the Congregation had for humanitarian needs around them. This behavior was, and continues to be a characteristic of the membership. This tradition of "caring" has been passed on from old member to new member: B'nai Israel must be involved in humanitarian endeavors.

The earliest recorded social action activity is found in 1886 when the Temple sent $50.00 to the Charleston congregation. The Congregation needed funds for repairs. In 1888 the Temple agreed to loan the "Russian Israelites of this community" a "sefer thora" (Torah scroll for reading during religious services. On numerous occasions, the Board authorized funds to assist numerous institutions, organizations and individuals in need, such as John Sealy Hospital in 1911 ($211.50), the Catholic orphanage in San Antonio in 1912, and the Southern Christian Leadership Conference in 1965, as a statement of concern on the racial strife in Selma, Alabama. In 1972, the Temple even considered, at the suggestion of congregant Charles Kuttner, withholding excise tax on the phone bill which was going for use to purchase weapons for the Viet Nam war. Two years later, the Temple's Contemporary Affairs Committee worked with voter registration on the Island and printed a booklet on the social service facilities available within the community.

In addition to assisting the community financially, Temple B'nai Israel were also made available to various groups. In 1890, the basement classrooms were opened, at no charge, to the Galveston Public Schools for classes. In 1891, the Helping Hand Society met at the Temple. In 1896, Sara A.Feist started a kindergarten and primary school program. On December 3, 1897, the Fourth Presbyterian Church began using the facilities for services. This continued until April, 1898.

In 1905, there were 164 members in the Congregation. When the City was raised in 1905 as a result of the Great 1900 Storm, Mrs.Eliza Kempner arranged for the raising of the Rabbinage, the home provided by the Temple for the Rabbi. Congregants were generous with the Temple and in turn, the Temple was able to provide assistance to others. On November 20, 1905, the Temple sent $1,800 to Russian Jewry, through the offices of the U.A.H.C. President, Samuel Woolner.

November 24, 1907, minutes note the establishment of the Jewish Immigrant Information Bureau with Henry Cohen as the Honorary Secretary, I.H.Kempner, I.Lovenberg, R.I.Cohen and Jos.Seinsheimer as the Committee, and M.D.Waldman as the Agent. The Bureau was known as the Galveston Plan and was specifically designed to shift immigrant entry to the Gulf Coast, thereby redirecting more settlement to the middle states. A wonderful display on this important piece of history can be found at the Texas Seaport Museum in Galveston. In that same year, 1917, the Temple began a two year fund raiser. This drive raised over $19,000 each year for the American Jewish Relief Committee for War Veterans. At the April 8, 1919, meeting of the Board, $250.00 was given to the American Pro-Falasha Committee.

In 1941, Captain Max Clark, the first Galvestonian to give his life for his country in WW II, resigned from the Congregation, because he was entering military service. The Board voted unanimously to keep him as a member without dues for as long as he desired. This same privilege was bestowed onto other members who entered the armed forces. In that same year, new by-laws were adopted by the Congregation.

During the war years, the Temple made its facilities available to the Jewish Welfare Board for parties for soldiers from Ft.Crockett and Camp Wallace. Interestingly, gambling was not permitted during these parties. The Temple was also the site of a Red Cross sewing unit. This was organized by Mrs.Zinn. Along with the sewing class, a Red Cross Canteen class was also held regularly in the building. In 1942, Civilian Defense Committee classes were held in the Vestry Room and the Temple collected funds and offered facilities to organize a Boy Scout Troop. In July of 1943, the Temple suffered major damage from a hurricane. The roof of the building was destroyed, pews were damaged, and the Community House used by the Red Cross as a chapter house was severely damaged. Early reports show the cost of repairs came to over $7,000.00.

Only a few ritual matters made it into the minutes. Again, it might be assumed that these matters were left to the rabbi's discretion, particularly after Dr.Cohen had been in his position for a number of years. On February 19, 1887, the General Assembly voted that all who enter the Temple must remove their hats. Until that time, there is no mention of whether or not the issue of head coverings were required. No other records indicate the reasoning behind this ritual decision, but Temple B'nai Israel was a Reform congregation. This clear by the congregation's attendance at U.A.H.C.conventions. This, in and of, itself would validate that the Temple perceived itself as Reform. It would seem logical to conclude that ritual practices, in concert with the Reform Movement's ideals, would be adopted.

In 1896, at the suggestion of Rabbi Cohen, the Congregation voted to adopt the Union Prayerbook. In 1912, the major notation in the minutes was a complaint by unnamed members that the binding on the new Union Prayer Books was very poor, as was the paper upon which it was printed. Sixty years later, that same complaint would be heard about the Gates of Prayer.

On November 27, 1904, Rabbi Cohen began Sunday night services and lectures. Rabbi Cohen changed the Friday night service from 6:00 p.m.to 8:00 p.m.on November 17, 1910. On January 11, 1920, Rabbi Cohen changed the *minhag* of B'nai Israel. Everyone at a service was now asked to rise for the reciting of *kaddish*. The new practice was explained as permitting all to share in the grief of friends and to provide them with support.

At the turn of the century Mrs.Eliza Kempner donated a home to the Temple for the rabbi. Henry Cohen was the first and only resident of that home. Over the years, this house and its successors would be referred to as the "Rabbinage." Most likely this was the first such a label had ever been given to a rabbi's home anywhere in the world.

The only mention of the 1900 storm is found on September 8, 1900, where the minutes report that a major storm had hit the island. Right after the storm, First Baptist Church held its services at B'nai Israel's building. Three years went by before the next recorded minutes are found. It is likely that this was due to a membership and rabbi much preoccupied with the rebuilding of the Island. As was noted earlier, this storm destroyed most of the Island and killed close to 8,000 islanders. The rebuilding of the city was accomplished through the efforts of a coordinating committee which included Rabbi Cohen, and three other members of the Temple: I. H. Kempner, M. Lasker and S. Levy. On March 15, 1903, Miss.M.Sandall sent a letter protesting the erection of an outhouse on Temple property. Though no record of the cause of the objection is reported, an explanation is not too difficult to suggest. Given the pleasant breezes that regularly prevail on the Island, a change in direction could easily reek havoc on the olfactory senses of a neighbor, particularly since it probably received more use than a family installation. As the outhouse issue may have been found difficult to discuss, so, too, may have been the reasons behind the objections to its being built. On March 2, 1904, the outhouse was removed.

In 1914, a one-way telephone was placed in the Temple for the convenience of the 174 members. At one of the meetings of the Board, it was suggested that the Temple merge with the Hebrew Benevolent Society, the organization responsible for the Reform Jewish community's cemetery. That motion would take over 65 years to pass. On April 11, 1923, the Temple Board voted in agreement with the U.A.H.C.that fermented wines were not necessary for sacramental purposes. Prohibition was still being enforced, so it might be speculated that this was done in support of the U.A.H.C. amendment.

From all reports, the Jews of Galveston have always been considered a part of the community. The churches in the city have, for the most part, worked well with the synagogues and have never excluded the rabbis from ministerial associations. Whether this is because the community is so small, or because of the shared problems of Island living, or whether it has been the awareness of the Jewish community of the feelings of the non-Jews, the results have been very positive.

The Jewish community has never sought to compromise their beliefs to gain approval or placate non-Jews. Rather their involvement and consideration was based on a concern for their fellow residents. Doing that which was right and proper was just a part of the warp and woof of Temple B'nai Israel. The result has been acceptance rather than unsettled tolerance.

The first mention of the Depression can be found in the minutes of the early 1930's. On March 9, 1932, it was reported that there were a number of meetings which were not held, due to the "Depression." In the same minutes it was reported that the attendance in religious school dropped to 132 and that this was due to the economic conditions. General membership in the Temple dropped to one hundred and seventy-six. In March of 1936, the first formal bulletin of the Temple was printed at 200 copies.

During World War II the business of the Temple continued. LeoSchornstein was still looking for a method to cool the Temple. Obviously the weather in Galveston included some days of insufferable heat and gather, even for important religious festivals, wasn't always so pleasant and air conditioning did yet commercially exist. On September 9, 1940, the Board passed a resolution that members would have to present tickets for the High Holy Day services. Along with this, no residents of the Island would be admitted without tickets and all non-residents would pay $5.00 per service. At the following Friday night service, it is reported that Rabbi Cohen announced that once again the Temple would not require tickets for admission in his congregation and that all would be welcome. So much for the tickets; and, to this day, no tickets are required for admission to High Holy Day services at the Temple. It was characteristic of Henry Cohen to take matters such as this, in to his own hands. Since he had been the rabbi of the Temple for fifty-two years, no one was going to seriously challenge him on this matter.

The 1950's saw several other events in the life of the Temple. Rabbi Leo Stillpass was authorized to send the minutes of the Congregation to the American Jewish Archives. Five years later, the rabbi began coming to the Board meetings on a regular basis. It is hard to characterize the relationship between the Board of Trustees and the rabbi. Though clearly an employee, the Rabbi of Temple B'nai Israel has traditionally been treated with great courtesy. This does not mean that the Board was just a rubber stamp for the rabbi. Even Henry Cohen had his ups and downs with Board members. What it does mean is that the Board was always willing to give the rabbi a chance. Board members have always listened to the concerns of the Rabbi and this was apparent even before he was entitled to attend all Board meetings. Because of this B'nai Israel has always been a desirable pulpit.

On July 17, 1957, $400.00 was loaned to start the Temple Academy which would become the pre-eminent nursery and kindergarten on the Island, and which was the creation of Rabbi Dreyfus. It was the first to admit students of different colors.

The conscience of Temple B'nai Israel is special. This "group consciousness" is passed on to new members through the expressed expectations of long time members. The relationship between the Board and Rabbi can best be explained by a popular but often resented comment, "that's how we do it here." Another way to phrase this relationship comes by way of the often used phrase in the Texas Legislature, "doing that which is right and proper." Just witnessing the actions and attitudes of the corporate body of Temple B'nai Israel explains the conscience of the Congregation. This conscience is manifest in the way the Board and the membership conduct the business of the Congregation. It can be seen in the waiving of dues for those in need. This was done without ever asking their names, while having them revealed only to the rabbi, the president and the treasurer. It is demonstrated in the Board paying for the *bar mitzvah* reception for a single, working parent's third child. This consciousness is obvious in the providing of free transportation for non-drivers to *shabbat* services, in establishing an integrated kindergarten, in providing funds to the Salvation Army for the homeless, and in many other humanitarian endeavors. In all these activities, the Temple has always remembered the value of a single human life and acted appropriately.

The first religious school was established on November 14, 1869, by Mr.Rosenspitz and he was paid $25 to run that school. The Board established a policy that there must be at least two Board members present each Sunday to assist in teaching. The students would pay for the books. These first books were approved by a committee and selected by Mr.Rosenspitz. In 1870, the minutes note the first Confirmation of the "Wenar, Schram and Gross children."

Clearly the Temple felt a need to be a part of the community and this religious community had Sunday schools. Instead of paralleling some *cheder* (three to five days after school classes at the synagogue) format and not having a school on Sunday, the Temple went ahead and established a Sunday program. This action permitted the Congregation to demonstrate that though Judaism was different, it could be a part of the community, a legitimate religious group. Though the Jewish Sunday School was not new nor unique to Galveston, it met the needs of the Jews on the Island.

Hebrew became an early requirement in the curriculum of the school. In 1877, a committee was appointed to oversee the program and it consisted of Mr.Halff and Mr.Bernstein. Mr.Marsberg was hired to teach Hebrew at $5.00.

Problems of space and classrooms were common with the religious school. In 1885, Rabbi Silverman arranged for the basement of the Temple to be divided into classrooms. This took care of the problem for a period of time.

No formal Sunday School curriculum is found in the records. From conversations with older members who attended the school, the courses they were taught included Jewish history, holidays, Hebrew, Bible with special attention to Psalms and Proverbs. As a matter of fact, children were required to know by heart Psalms 1, 8, 15 and 23 by the fifth grade as well as several Proverbs. In addition, Rabbi Cohen used *Religion and Morals, A Short Catechism For The Use Of Jewish Youth,* a text written by Rev.J Strauss, PhD., M.A. This book was published in London, England in 1895. Questions and answers from the text were committed to memory by all his confirmands.

In 1903, Rabbi Cohen began using his famous lantern slides of the Bible and the Holy Land. These were created with the assistance of Mr.J.R.Cox who worked for the Brush Electric Light and Power Company. He purchased his slides from L.M.Price, an optician in Cincinnati, Ohio, at a cost of $.50 per slide with a 20 percent discount for clergy.

Dr. Cohen used to have the slides shone from one end of the basement social hall against the wall at the other end. The shamas, Yiddish term for custodian of the building, would show the slides and when Dr. Cohen wanted him to change the slide, he loudly tapped a tall staff on the floor and that was the signal to switch.

Like these first Sunday school students, so in 1917, children of members of the Orthodox Congregation were students at "Henry Cohen's religious school." It was suggested by the Board that the families of these children should be asked to contribute to the school. Rabbi Cohen opposed this proposal. He felt it would keep the children away because their parents would see it as formally supporting Reform. Interestingly enough, of the two hundred children in the school, one hundred and sixty came from homes of the Orthodox congregation. The motion for students to contribute to Sunday School was dropped. In spite of this, the school was closed for over six weeks due to an influenza epidemic, the following year, 1918.

It is historically important to understand why the Religious School of Temple B'nai Israel was used by members of the Orthodox community. Though the parents felt their synagogue was able to provide the necessary instruction in Hebrew and *davenen,* the Americanized understanding of

Judaism was beyond their immigrant knowledge. Dr.Cohen could be trusted to teach their children about American Jewry without alienating them from their parents' approach to Judaism.

Though there was a sizeable Orthodox community on the Island, there was never a single, large influx of Eastern European Jews. Immigrants who arrived through the Galveston Plan generally did not settle in Galveston. The Eastern European Jews came on their own to the States because they had relatives, friends or business offers.

In the late 1890's, there was the Young Men's Hebrew Association composed of Russian Jews and the Hebrew Orthodox Benevolent Association established at the turn of the century and made up of Austro-Hungarian Jews. Up until these two groups merged in 1930 into Congregation Beth Jacob, the religious school was conducted on weekdays in the Orthodox mode and on Sundays at Dr.Cohen's congregation. For Henry Cohen, Jews were Jews regardless of their affiliation and they were all entitled to an education. This resulted was in a tolerance for each other, be it Reform or Orthodox. Because of this tolerance, the country of origin never arose as an issue.

In 1919, the Orthodox congregation became large enough to hire their own teacher and the enrollment of the Temple's school dropped significantly. Off and on from 1900 to 1974, the enrollment records of the Congregation were recorded.

In addition to providing education for the children of the Temple, programs were also held for the edification of the adult membership. Most of these programs consisted of either of Sunday evening lectures by Henry Cohen or guest speakers. These programs were attended by non-Jews as well as Jews and were not only on Jewish topics but on current issues as well. For a time, there was established a "Temple Society" which organized some of these lectures. Clearly in the last days of the late 1800's and the early days of the 1900's people were used to listening to lectures, and the Temple was in the forefront of organizing such edifying activities. The modern manifestations of these early programs are the Clergy Institute started by Rabbi Dreyfus, the Hochman/Perlman Scholar in Residence funded by Ms. Hanah Hochman and organized by Rabbi Martin Levy and the Reiswerg Memorial Lectures organized by Rabbi Kessler and funded by Sara and Harold Levy. Art was also a part of the Congregations heritage. For many years in the 1960's and 1970's, the Temple held the major art auction in Galveston. Then in 1972, Edna Levin and her daughter, Gerry Hornstein, completed needlepoint Torah covers and ark backdrop which were in turn given by Edna's mother-in-law, Jeannette Lipson.

Among the several programs introduced at the Temple in this period was a monthly pot-luck dinner following the second Friday night service of the month; a Black-White *seder* between the

Temple and African American churches; an annual avocation auction; and during the Galveston Dicken's weekend the Temple members dressed in appropriate garb and conducted an 1868 Sabbath service from England.

The story of the cemeteries used by the many of the members of B'nai Israel rightly belongs a history of the Hebrew Benevolent Society. The Hebrew Benevolent Society, organized in 1865, is the oldest Jewish organization in Galveston and was formed to provide for the burial of Jews. In the 1970's the Society, made up of members of B'nai Israel, turned its assets over to the Temple and the name of the Society was preserved as a committee of the Congregation. In as much as the Hebrew Benevolent Society cemetery on Broadway was full, a new cemetery was established by the Temple on T ½ and 61st Street.

Over the recent years members have stepped forward to support the Temple and they, too, have left a significant mark upon the Congregation. In 1965 funds were left by the Stein and Wagg families for a new memorial plaque in the Sanctuary. Then in that same year the David Nathan Fund was established for the beautification of the pulpit and the purchase of Torahs. Elton Lipnick of Houston established the Lipnick Religious School Fund. This fund provides camp scholarships and programs for the students of the Religious School, annually. Marlene Nathan Meyerson provided funds for the refurbishing of the Temple classrooms in honor of her parents, Tillie and David Nathan. The large, unused backyard of the Temple was converted into a playground for the children of Temple members through the generosity of Drs. Carla and Michael Brandon in honor his parents Drs. Sylvan and Elizabeth Brandon. Dr. Abe Levy established the Abe and Peggy Levy Goodworks Fund which has been supported by his niece Marilyn McFatridge and her husband, Keith. In addition, Dr. Ray Ogra created a good works fund in honor of his wife and Mrs. Marilyn March established the same in honor of her father. In order to maintain continuity, the Temple took over the Predecki Fund, a small educational fund to cover college expenses and created by past members of the Temple.

The Temple has been fortunate to benefit from the foresight of its early members who established an endowment fund encouraged by David Nathan during this presidency; this particularly offsets those operating expenses, not covered by dues and gifts. The Temple has greatly benefited from significant gifts to the endowment fund by the Harris and Eliza Kempner Fund, Mr. E. R. Thompson, Jr., Mr. and Mrs. Robert Lynch, Mr. and Mrs. Ronnie Yambra, Mrs. Harris L. (Ruth) Kempner, Sr., Mr. and Mrs. Adrian Levy, Sr. and Mrs. Lewis (Frances Kay) Harris and Mr. and Dr. Dominick Sasser, and Mr. and Mrs. Marvin Stein. The Congregation would not be solvent as it is were not for the generosity of these folk and others like these.

The Rabbis

Temple B'nai Israel has a rich and wonderful history. Much of this amazing history rotates around the Temple's Rabbis, specifically Dr. Henry Cohen. Cohen's presence permeates the pages of the minutes of the Congregation. Much of this history has also been recorded recorded in *The Man Who Stayed in Texas* by H. Cohen and A. Nathan, *Henry Cohen: Messenger of the Lord* by Stanley Dreyfus, and *Henry Cohen: The Life of a Frontier Rabbi* by Jimmy Kessler.

In August of 1868 I.Frank, the first President of the new Temple B'nai Israel, appointed a committee of himself, I.Wenar and S.E.Loeb to make arrangements for the coming holidays. At their September 16, 1868, meeting, the committee was authorized to pay no more than $50 per month for a "shamas", janitor or *general fact totum* for those holidays. On March 14, 1869, arrangements were made for Passover and fees for the meal were set at $1.00 for males, $.50 for ladies and families, and $2.50 for non-members. $28.00 was charged for rental of Wenar

Hall and $15.00 was charged by I.B.Root and Son for chairs.

On May 23, 1869, the Executive Committee recommended to the General Assembly of the Congregation that the President or someone "compeitent" be authorized that marriages be done "according to the Mosaic tradition." The first Shamas was a man named Padusky. He was engaged for the 1869 holidays at $25.00. Mr.A.Allen rented the Goldstein building for those services and the Galveston Glee Club served as the choir. Mr.Krausser served as the "musical operator."

The first mention in the Temple minutes of the first Rabbi is not clear, but it is obvious there was an initial clergy leader. On November 14, 1869, the minutes record, "Mr.Rosenspitz sent a letter asking for funds to set up a Sunday School." How and why Mr.Rosenspitz came to Galveston is not recorded. It was not until the following year, March 27, 1870, that Mr.Rosenspitz was engaged "as minister at $50 per month." At that same meeting, he was loaned $300 at 12% interest to rent rooms for a school and secure a hall to hold religious services. It is assumed that Mr. Rosenspitz kept any fees collected for the school and used them to repay the note, even though this was never mentioned in the minutes.

For some unknown reason, the Executive Committee dismissed Mr. Rosenspitz as teacher of the Hebrew Sunday School that the Board declared to be a part of B'nai Israel. They then authorized Mrs.I.(L.C.)Harby to set up another school in the Temperance Hall. This same building would be used in 1870 for the High Holy Days.

Upon leaving Galveston, Rabbi Alexander Rosenspitz went to Omaha, Nebraska. There he served Congregation Israel and conducted their first Confirmation service. He later returned to Texas where he served as Rabbi in San Antonio. From Texas, Rabbi Rosenspitz moved to Portland, Oregon where he served Congregation Beth Israel from 1881 to 1884.

In the absence of a minister, in 1870 I.E.Loeb officiated at High Holy Day services. Congregation members were charged $1.00 for admission to High Holy Day services and $5.00 was charged for non-members.

In 1871, the Executive Committee authorized Messrs.Labatt, Kory and Frank to draw up duties and procedures for a shamas. The following were approved by the Board:a) the shamas would draw a salary of $30.00 per month; b) open building on Friday night and Saturday morning, for all holidays and upon order of the President; c) keep the building clean and tend to the lights daily and check with the President on requirements; d) notify all officers and members of meetings, attend all meetings and collect all monies due the Temple; e) establish a *chevra kadisha* and arrange its ministrations that in case of a death of a member or family member, and assist in washing the body; and, f) the President may suspend him from work or pay, but it required a 2/3 vote of the Board to sustain the action. By March of 1871, the salary was raised to $50 per month.

The Congregation began advertising in the *Israelite* and *Messenger* for a minister to be a "lecturer, hasan, and leader" on January 29, 1871. The following applied for the position:Rev.A.S.Bittelheim, Richmond; Rev.I.Wechsler, Columbus, Ohio; Rev.Charles Newburgh, Fasorell Courthouse, Virginia; Rev.Abraham Blum, Augusta, Georgia; Rev.E.B.M.Browne, Madison, Wisconsin; and Rev.S.A.Meyers, New York. The position was offered to Rev.Blum on a trial visit. The Temple agreed to pay his traveling expenses "should he 'suit' the membership." On June 11, 1871, Mr.Blum was hired as Rabbi for one year.

Rabbi Blum arrived in time to dedicate the new synagogue on May 15, 1871. While serving the Temple, Blum married Hannah Henriques of New Orleans. During the fifteen years of his service, Rabbi Blum enhanced the activity of the Hebrew Young Men's Literary Association, the religious school and the theatrical activities of the Congregtion. Among his more notable achievements was his receipt of his M.D.degree in 1879 from the Medical College of Galveston while serving the Temple. In 1880, Blum offered to serve small U.A.H.C. congregations around Galveston.

In 1871. the minutes show that after selecting a Rabbi, the Board turned again to the need for a shamas. M.A.Seifort, of New Orleans, A.Potosky, of Galveston and M.Woolf, of Galveston, applied for the job at $30.00 per month. The job was offered to Mr.Woolf on May 21, 1871. Two days later, Mr.Woolf requested more money. The Board raised his salary to $50.00, if he agreed to handle Consecration as of June. On May 29, 1871, the minutes record that Mr.Epstein applied for the post of shamas. Mr.Isaac Cohen was elected shamas in June to replace Mr. Woolf at a salary of $40.00 per month. Interestingly enough, Mr. Cohen had a stipulation that he did not have to clean the classrooms. In July, however, Mr.Cohen had the cleaning of classrooms added to his duties. On May 24, 1874, Mr.Hambert Cahn was elected shamas and was told to wear a black suit while he was on duty.

On October 9, 1871, Rabbi Blum was granted permission by the Board to leave the city to perform a wedding for Mr.Halff in Victoria provided he was back in time to conduct services. On February 18, 1872, Rabbi Blum was rehired for one year (May, 1872-1873) at $1,800.00. The decrease in pay was due to a shortage of money in the Temple. However, he was authorized to use the building gratis for educational purposes and any funds raised he could keep. In addition, the parents were urged to send their children to his school.

In 1873, Rev.Blum was reelected for one more year. In November of that year, he proposed to the Board that he begin delivering lectures in English at each service. The Board asked him to refrain from doing so for the time being. Rev.Blum was then unanimously elected in 1874 for two years.

The Temple changed shamases again and then had to fire the newly hired shamas in May, 1874, because of "missing money."

In November, 1875, I.W.Frank moved to advertise for a "minister who not only knew the service and would use *minhag America,* the new Reform prayerbook, but also who could speak English." The ad read, "the annual election of a minister for Congregation B'nai Israel of Galveston, Texas to serve for one year from the first of May, 1876 will take place on Sunday, February 20, 1876. Applications for the position are solicited from such as are fully compitent to conduct religious services according to *minhag America,* deliver English lectures and superintend a Hebrew and Sunday school. Salary - $2,100 per annum, no expenses paid. Address - M.Kopperl, President."

By December, three applications were received fromDr.Louis Aton, Albany; Dr.Larner, Memphis; and Dr.Gerstman, St.Joseph. A Dr.Fluegel wrote asking for more inducements to come, but the Board wrote that there were none. In addition, applications were received from Rev.Max Moses, of New Orleans, and Rev.J.M.De Sola, of New York. At the February 20, 1876 Board meeting, four names were submitted - Moses, Gerstmann, and De Sola with

Blum added at the last minute. Blum received a majority vote and was reelected for another year. For the next eight years, Rev.Blum was reelected Rabbi of the Congregation. During these years, the Temple required the Rabbi to conduct services at 6:00 p.m.on Friday night and at 10:00 a.m.on Saturday morning. The shamas was instructed to keep people quiet during services. The first choir committee was created on October 19, 1876, and it consisted of members Halff, Bernstein and Lovenberg.

Abraham Blum was born in 1843 in Gutzenheim in Alsace in northeastern France. Though he desired to study at the Paris Rabbinical Seminary, he had to settle for ordination from the Rabbinical School at Niederbronn. There he also received a license as a *mohel* (ritual circumciser) and a *shochet* (ritual animal slaughterer). He arrived in the United Statesin 1868 where he became the Rabbi in Dayton, Ohio. After leaving Dayton, Blum went to Augusta, Georgia, and then in 1871, he came to Galveston where he served as Rabbi until 1885. When Blum left Galveston, due to failing health, he did not permanently leave the Rabbinate. Over the next few years, he served pulpits in Sacramento, Los Angeles, San Bernardino, and San Francisco. In 1911, he became the Chaplain of the New York City Police Department where he worked closely with his successor, Rabbi Joseph Silverman who by that time had become Rabbi of Temple Emanu El. Rabbi Blum died on August 6, 1921.

In November, the Board began to advertise for another Rabbi, but this time noted that all candidates would have to travel to visit at their own expense. After several months, Rabbi Dr.Joseph Silverman was hired on May 17, 1885. In 1886, Rev.Silverman was reelected for three years.

Rabbi Silverman, born in Cincinnati in 1860, was ordained at the Hebrew Union College in 1884. Prior to coming to Galveston, he served one year in Dallas at Temple Emanu El.During his first year in Galveston, Silverman married Henrietta Bloch. He was the first of the single Rabbis to come and marry a Galveston woman within the first year. The smoothness of acceptance of the new Rabbi came to an abrupt end. The Board allowed Rabbi Silverman's to visit New York and to speak at Temple Emanu El. On January 29, 1888, Emanu El wrote saying Silverman had been elected "Junior Minister". The Board of Emanu El asked the Board of B'nai Israel to release him from his contract as of February 20, 1888. The Board voted to grant the request with regret, but added a wish for happiness on his "promotion." The idea of B'nai Israel being a "stepping stone" for Rabbis began with this action and this practice continued in the mind of many future clergy.

Applications for the next Rabbi were received from Rev.H.Cohen, of Woodville, Mississippi, Rabbi E.L.Hess, of Shreveport, Louisiana, Rabbi L.Freudenthal, of Des Moines, Iowa, and Rabbi G.E.Harfield, of Richmond, Virginia.

On May 13, 1888, Henry Cohen was elected Rabbi, and thus began a 64-year relationship between Rabbi and congregation.Leo N.Levi was president of the Congregation at that time. There is a story passed down orally, though not in the minutes, that Henry Cohen stuttered. When asked how he could have hired such a Rabbi, Levi is reported to have said that "we will get used to it." The story continues. Cohen spent years overcoming his disability by walking along the beach and practicing the delivery of his sermons to the waves with small pebbles in his mouth. In addition, the Congregation learned to understand the British accent Cohen maintained throughout his life. More than just a relationship, it was a marriage. Galvestonians would see Dr.Cohen become "the" minister on the Island, and "the" Rabbi of Texas.

Some of the information taken from the minutes and used in books on Dr. Cohen has been embellished, while other interesting bits of information have never been printed. Here are a few interesting notes about Dr. Cohen.

Henry Cohen was born in London, England, on April 7, 1862. His early studies took place at Jew's Hospital where traditional Jewish practices were taught. Later he attained the title of "Minister" from Jews College in London. In 1881 Henry and his brother, Mark, went to the Capetown Colony where he learned Zulu dialects and visited the country. In 1884 Cohen returned to England where he was persuaded by Dr.Herman Adler, President of Jews College, to assume the duties of assistant Reader in the Synagogue of Amalgamated Israelites in Kingston, Jamaica. After one year, Cohen left Kingston for Woodville, Mississippi, where he stayed until 1888. After this, he came to Galveston Island.

Rabbi Cohen did not begin on a propitious note. Upon his arrival in Galveston, he was granted a leave of absence from the pulpit due to ill health. Save for periodic disputes about salary, Rabbi Cohen was continually rehired by the Congregation without much controversy. After his first year, he married Molly Levy, a local Galveston girl, and they had two children. In his second year, he began two-month vacations each summer. This practice of taking a two-month vacation continued throughout his tenure. His favorite vacation location was the Crazy Wells Hotel in Mineral Wells, Texas. He, like many other Texans, went to this out of the way location because of the natural mineral springs and baths.

In September, 1889, he arranged for a buzzer to signal the choir when he wanted them to sing. That same year, the Kempner family gave a home to the Congregation for the Rabbi's use. It became known among Rabbis throughout the nation as the "Rabbinage." Sewage was hooked up to the house in 1903 at a cost of $39.95. In 1897, the Board voted to replace the shofar (ram's horn) with the organ making the sounds for the High Holy Days. Cohen took no heed of this action, and continued to have the shofar sounded throughout his tenure. On May 15, 1898, upon the recommendation of Dr.Cohen, 136 Union Prayer Books were ordered at a cost of $109.20.

Rabbi Cohen was "elected Rabbi of this Congregation during the term of his life at his will" on May 15, 1904. Along with this, in the early 1900's, Rabbi Cohen removed his head covering at services and began to ask members to follow suit. In addition, in 1944 he opposed the use of the then new Union Prayer Book but ultimately acquiesced. He said he was satisfied with the old one. Against his desires, in December of 1949, services on Friday night were switched from 6:00 PM to 8:00 PM. Cohen preferred the 6:00 PM because the earlier time allowed families to have Sabbath supers together. Temple history and folklore tell us that he began his services with the strike of the 6:00 PM bells of Trinity Episcopal Church, across from the Temple, and was at his supper table a few blocks from the Temple in time to hear the 7:00 PM bells of Trinity.

Among the many activities for which Henry Cohen was known, one of the most often cited was his involvement with the "Galveston Movement". The actual name for this project, started by Jacob Schiff and others in New York, was the Jewish Immigrant's Information Bureau. The goal of this project was to help settle the new wave of European immigrants who were fleeing the Russian pogroms of Czars Alexander III and

Nicholas II, in other parts of the United States and who would have normally settled in the already crowded streets of New York City. Henry Cohen was asked to help meet the boats at the port of Galveston. He was also asked to get the new arrivals through the immigration procedures, and arrange for their passage to new homes in other locales. As a result of Rabbi Cohen's Herculean efforts, many Jews found new lives. Along with this, these once unsure immigrants had wonderful memories of a Rabbi who wrote notes on his shirt cuffs and who helped them settle in this land of freedom.

Beginning in 1917, Rabbi Cohen was also periodically serving the orthodox community of Galveston. In 1924 he was given a Doctor of Jewish Laws degree by the Hebrew Union College in Cincinnati. On several occasions, the Congregation offered to provide Rabbi Cohen with an assistant Rabbi, but he refused each time. In 1940, Cohen had recorded in the minutes, for the first time, thoughts on the time-place-setting in which the Jews then found themselves.He wrote, "Jewish affairs have changed immeasurably in the last few years. We have something to fall back upon and the only thing we can fall back upon is our dignity as Jews. What saves us is our own pride in our faith which we can only learn in the synagogue. That we still walk the earth after 5,000 years of persecution is proof of such."

On September 12, 1949, Rabbi Cohen

announced his retirement. The Board agreed to grant retirement at his current salary of $7,950 and life time use of the Rabbinage for him and Molly. Rabbi Cohen died on June 12, 1952.

On January 2, 1950, Leo Stillpass was elected. Rabbi Stillpass was born in Fort Wayne, Indiana in 1917 and was ordained at the Hebrew Union College in 1943. Prior to coming to Galveston, he had been a Naval Chaplain during World War II. At his request, Mrs.Mathilde Colby was hired as Secretary to the Rabbi. A house was rented for Rabbi Stillpass at 4702 N 1/2 for $85.00 per month. Rabbi Stillpass was reelected in 1952 and in 1954. Rabbi Stillpass was adored by the children of the Temple. After leaving Galveston, he went on to serve other congregations and passed away in 1978.

Rabbi Stillpass was Rabbi during the building of the new Temple on Avenue O. Above the ark in the new building, as in every synagogue, is an eternal light. The light in B'nai Israel is in the shape of two hands forming the Hebrew letter "shin". This is historically how the Levitical priests held their hands to bless the Jewish people in the Temple in Jerusalem. The large hands on the B'nai Israel pulpit were cast from a drawing of Rabbi Stillpass's hands.

Dr.A.Stanley Dreyfus was named Rabbi of Temple B'nai Israel on January 11, 1956. Rabbi Dreyfus was born in Youngstown, Ohio. He received his ordination and doctorate in philosophy from the Hebrew Union College. Prior to coming to Galveston, he served on the faculty of the Hebrew Union College. He also served as Rabbi of the United Hebrew Congregation in Terre Haute, Indiana as well as Visiting Minister of West London Synagogue in London, England. Of the many major achievements during his years in Galveston, two stand the test of time. Rabbi Dreyfus helped establish the Temple Academy that was housed for several years in the Temple itself. The Academy was a nursery/kindergarten program for children of every race and creed, and which had as its one goal excellence in education. Dreyfus's other achievement was the first "Clergy Institute" program in Texas. Every other year, the Temple brought in a well known Jewish scholar to speak to the clergy of all denominations in the area. The Sisterhood of the Temple provided breakfast and lunch while individual members offset the expenses of the program.

Rabbi Dreyfus was widely respected in the community and apparently sought after as a candidate for other pulpits. As a matter of fact, the Board approved a three-week leave in 1957 so that he could visit the United Progressive Jewish Congregation of South Africa which was seeking a new Rabbi.Rabbi Dreyfus also noted the need for good community relations. He obtained the Board's support for Congregational payment for the Rabbi's yearly dues to Rotary as well as the weekly costs. Though a motion was passed in 1957 to secure a home for the Rabbi, it was not until May 20, 1959, that the Ben Clark residence at 4602 Woodrow was purchased for $33,000. Actually, the house came into the hands of the Congregation through the good offices of the the Kempner family who owned the United States National Bank of Galveston. On January 8, 1962, the Board approved a motion that the Rabbi would attend all Board meetings except when asked to be absent by the President.

Rabbi Dreyfus was given a seven-year contract on February 11, 1963. Two years later, he resigned from the pulpit to move to Brooklyn where he became the Rabbi of Union Temple. From there, he would move on to become Director of Placement for the Central Conference of American Rabbis.

There were three candidates in 1965 interested in replacing Rabbi Dreyfus. Rabbi Saul Besser, who decided to remain in Dallas, Rabbi Chaim Stern and Rabbi Louis Firestein. As the Board had not decided in time for the High Holy Days, they engaged Rabbi Sol Kaplan, then Regional Director of the U.A.H.C., to conduct those services.

Robert Blinder was elected Rabbi of B'nai Israel on July 25, 1965. His first contract was for two years and he assumed the pulpit on November 1, 1965. Rabbi Blinder was a man of commitment and he made religious and intellectual demands upon the membership. He was ordained at the Hebrew Union College in 1957. After his tenure in Galveston, he went on to a private practice in counseling as well as service to Genesis:A Synagogue for Our Time in St.Louis, Missouri. In 1966 he introduced the first *selichot* service (a midnight service of repentance weeks before the High Holy Days) at the Temple. In May, 1969, Rabbi Blinder left the Temple to become a member of the staff of the U.A.H.C.

Sam Stahl came to Galveston after serving the military as a chaplain. Having graduated with honors from the Hebrew Union College in 1967, Rabbi Stahl also served congregations in Ishpeming, Michigan, Charleroi, Pennsylvania, and Mansfield, Ohio. He was Rabbi of the Temple from 1969 until 1976. During his tenure, the Temple choir and the Congregation's status in the community were greatly enhanced. He, too, left his contract early for Temple Beth El in San Antonio. The recipient of a doctorate from the Hebrew Union College, Rabbi Stahl was also the Editor of the *The Journal of Reform Judaism*.

On May 10, 1976, Rabbi Jimmy Kessler was elected Rabbi of the Temple. Rabbi Kessler wasthe first native Texan to assume the leadership of Henry Cohen's Congregation. After completing his studies at the Hebrew Union College-Jewish Institute of Religion in Cincinnati, he graduated as the outstanding senior. Before coming to B'nai Israel of Galveston, Rabbi Kessler's first pulpit was the B'nai B'rith Hillel Foundation at the University of Texas in Austin. Like Cohen and Silverman, Kessler came to Galveston single.

In 1977 the "fatal matrimonial malady" befell Kessler when, within one year, married a Galveston girl, Shelley Gail Nussenblatt, a BOI. Kessler stayed at B'nai Israel from 1976 through 1981.

During Kessler's first tenure, he established the weekly Sabbath family covered dish dinners, the Sabbath morning study group following services and the increased use of readers for the holy day services. Rabbi Kessler also founded the Texas Jewish Historical Society and served as its first president. During his first five years in Galveston, Kessler served as president of the Galveston Ministerial Association, served on the Institutional Review Board of UTMB, and was on the boards of the American Red Cross, the Mental Health Mental Retardation Association and the Family Service Center. Kessler was selected as the first chair of the Church Relations Advisory Board to the Department of Human Resources of the State of Texas.

Under mutually pleasant conditions, Rabbi Kessler left Galveston in 1981 for Austin. From 1981 to 1988, he served as the part-time Rabbi of the Jewish community in Victoria, Texas. From 1988 to 1989, he served as the Rabbi of the Jewish Temple in Alexandria, Louisiana.

In 1981, Alan Greenbaum came to B'nai Israel and remained as Rabbi through 1984. During his tenure, Galveston suffered signficiant damage from Hurricane Alicia. In 1985, Rabbi

Martin Levy assumed the pulpit and served through 1989.

In 1989, Rabbi Kessler was called back to Congregation B'nai Israel. While away from Galveston, the Rabbi and his wife Shelley had two children: Andy Joshua and Jenny Ann. In addition, Kessler obtained his Doctor of Hebrew Letters degree from the Hebrew Union College - Jewish Institute of Religion in Los Angeles with a major in Texas Jewish History. He also received an honorary Doctor of Divinity from HUC-JIR in 1997. During his current tenure, Kessler was elected to the Philosophical Society of Texas, only the fifth Rabbi to ever be a member since 1836, joining a list that included Henry Cohen. In addition, Kessler has returned to serve on the Institutional Review Boards of UTMB and St. Mary's Hospital, the boards of Galveston Historical Foundation, the Family Service Center, Children's Center, the Wesley Foundation, Edgewater Retirement Center, the 1894 Grand Opera House, Independence Manor, St. Vincent's House, Jesse Tree (one of its three founders), United Way, and as president of the Galveston Ministerial Association. Dr. Kessler also teaches at Galveston College and in the Institute of Medical Humanities at UTMB. In 1992, Rabbi Kessler was extended a "till retirement" contract with the congregation, and in 1996 he has selected as a Trustee of the Harris and Eliza Kempner Fund and the Abe and Peggy Levy

Foundation. In honor of Rabbi Kessler's service as the Jewish chaplain at UTMB, Temple B'nai Israel contributed three stained glass windows in his honor for the UTMB chapel.

Psalm 16:5-6 records, "The Lord is my chosen portion and my cup; thou holdest my lot. The line has fallen for me in pleasant places; yea, I have a goodly heritage." In unique ways, each of the Rabbis who have served Temple B'nai Israel would apply this verse to their tenure. Though they have had impact upon the membership, the character of the Congregation and the Island have surely had their impact upon these men. In all, one wants to think, they both have come out ahead.

An Overview

The historical period of these several pages covers one hundred and thirty six years. Congregation B'nai Israel is still going strong, and its future history is yet to be recorded. Entwined with the past of B'nai Israel is the history of Galveston Island and the state of Texas.

The history of Texas, of Galveston and of B'nai Israel have many similarities. Each sprung from a pioneer spirit that responded to feelings and desires for freedom and opportunity. Texas is, by its very existence, a statement of freedom for people of European stock. Those who sought to live within its borders found the potential for rights denied to them in other locales. Clearly lives were given to secure those freedoms, but the potential for achievement was the enticement for their involvement. As a result, there arose and still exists a tenacious abandon of all restraint in the maintenance of that freedom. In addition, Texas was a frontier of opportunity from its first settlement. Though fortunes were made and lost on numerous occasions, the fact that there existed the possibility served as well as the enticement for risk. Texas was a breeding ground for entrepreneurs.

Jews from Europe were a part of those who came to help in the taming of the new land. Some came as *conversos* who could not identify as Jews but who were permitted to come because of their business acumen. Others came in covered wagons under the aegis of grants to Anglos who tried to live under Mexican rule. And still others answered the call of those who would free the land from rulers who sought to limit rights and opportunities. Texas welcomed them all and each found a home.

As the first Texans sought to free themselves from Mexican bondage, they also sought to establish a civilization in the midst of the new land. Galveston, Texas, clearly was an appropriate early location for a piece of that civilization. Though it was an island and subject to the dangers of weather and water, it provided an excellent port on its leeward side and a quiet bay adjoining the mainland.

Intimately involved with the warp and woof of the Island were the Jewish residents. Many of the first Jewish settlers lived on Snake Island. These immigrants who escaped European anti-semitism, sought the very same goals as their non-Jewish neighbors. Some made fortunes and of them, some lost all. Others settled into a life style that permitted them to establish a business and raise a family within means that could easily be characterized as successful. Freedom and opportunity were readily available to the Jews of Galveston and many took advantage of both.

In spite of the community involvement, it took a bit of outside prodding to move the Jewish residents to formally establish a synagogue. Though it is certainly logical to assume that the Jewish residents met for services long before 1868, it was not until then that Congregation B'nai Israel was chartered by the state. Records do not show the religious background of the early members of the congregation. What is interesting to note is that they established a Reform temple and not an Orthodox shul like Houston's Congregation Beth Israel, which was the first chartered synagogue in 1854. Congregation B'nai Israel became a charter member of the Union of American Hebrew Congregations in 1873 and has remained in the mainstreem of Reform ever since its establishment.

Over the one hundred plus years, Congregation B'nai Israel has been a known presence on the Island. Due to its members, their contributions, its rabbis and their contributions, the Temple has always been actively involved in almost everything that has happened in Galveston. Mayors, city council members, board chairpersons, presidents of the medical school, bank presidents and directors, insurance company presidents and directors, port directors, school board presidents and members, and numerous other leadership positions have been held by members of Temple B'nai Israel. In each position, they have in one way or another represented not only their views but the Jewish community as well, and the Temple in particular.

No discussion or summary of Congregation B'nai Israel can be concluded without mentioning the name of Henry Cohen. Any Congregation served by a rabbi for over 60 years, can't help but be influenced by that personality. Just as members were involved in the city, so, too, was Dr.Cohen. As early generations might have been examples for him in their communal participation, so was he an example for later generations. Cohen set a pattern that the entire Jewish community copied for decades, even after his death.

Interestingly, the membership of the Congregation has not varied greatly in its one hundred year plus existence. During its beginning years, the Congregation grew to over 100 member families but less than 200, and has remained such. In spite of the flow of residents on and off the Island, there has been a core of permanent residents who have always been a part of the fabric of the Temple. As a result, the Temple has not suffered debilitating fluctuations in membership.

As the years have passed, Congregation B'nai Israel has remained a viable synagogue and a respected presence in Galveston. It is clear from the records that for many it had a significant influence. Not only did it respond to their religious needs, but also had an impact on the social, cultural, educational, ethical and moral fabric of their lives. For others, the Temple has simply been a place to belong, and the rabbi, a professional to use.

B.O.I.'s are tenacious, persistent, expressive and devoted to the preservation of the outstanding heritage which is Galveston, Texas. Temple B'nai Israel is no exception. The history of the Temple supports that contention. There is no reason to assume that anything will be different when the Temple celebrates its two hundreth and thirty-sixth year.

B'nai Israel is similar to an *etz chayim* (tree of life). Its roots are deep and strong. Its branches extend far and wide. Its leaves provide shade and its supporters have found peace of spirit. Having passed *mea v'esrim* (one hundred and twenty), it is fair to assume that one hundred and twenty years from now, this B.O.I.will still have the sand between her toes and the Jewish community, Galveston and Texas will still be blessed by her presence.

B'nai Israel pulpit, circa 1920s.

*B'nai Israel Com-
munity House,
24th and Avenue I.*

*Dr. Henry Cohen,
circa 1950s.*

B'nai Israel Dicken's Program, 1994.

Temple B'nai Israel, 2001.

B'nai Israel Chapel, 2003.

B'nai Israel Sanctuary, 2003.

Texas: A Haven for Entrepreneurs

The history of Texas is a history of entrepreneurship. To an untamed land came questers of fortune and freedom who identified, organized, managed and assumed the necessary risks to achieve their goals. This was true of the Jewish pioneers as well as their non-Jewish co-settlers.

Found in the records of the early Colonial Period and the Republic are numerous names presumed to be Jewish. Though identifying their "Jewishness" is at times difficult, their presence as Jews was in some manner recognized, otherwise such information would not be available today.

The most difficult period in which to identify Jews is the Colonial Period of Mexico during which time Texas was a part of Nueva Espana. Many of the records are based upon Inquisition documents or inferences from them. Though this leaves much room for question, it is still desirable to mention those to whom history and tradition have assigned the label. According to Seymour B.Liebman, four Jews were listed in the auto de fe of 1528. Two of these, Hernando Alonso and Gonzalo de Morales were conquistadors with Cortes. There is some question about Gaspar Castano de Sosa whose name appears in early records of Nueva Leon, but there is no question as to the Jewish identity of Luis de Carvajal, el mozo (d.1596). As Martin Cohen has noted in his book, *Martyr*, this nephew of the Governor of Tamalipas left one of the few written works by a Jew of that time.

Though there were Jews in *Nueva Espana* with the *conquistadores,* the first organized Jewish community in what became the United States was in New Amsterdam. Others followed this initial group to different colonies in pre-Revolutionary America. Each Jewish enclave faced not only the dangers of the frontier, but the trials concomitant with their efforts to obtain acceptance from their fellow settlers.

There is discernible in each of the waves of Jewish immigration, a similarity of goals. They established synagogues and cemeteries not only to meet their needs, but also to fit in with the churches and cemeteries of their neighbors. As the communities grew and there were demands for more organized response, formalization of the community structure began.

At the beginning of the nineteenth century, one finds New Orleans, Louisville, St.Louis, Cincinnati, Cleveland, Montgomery, Nacogdoches and Galveston counting Jews amongst their residents. Clearly one of the motivating enticements for movement to these outposts was the economic potential. In addition, of course, Jews came for the freedoms and opportunities they did not enjoy in their countries of origin.

According to one of the conventional divisions of Jewish immigration, the second wave from Germany ran from 1840-1880. Though they were perceived as typifying a lower socio-economic level than the first immigrants of Spanish origin, nonetheless, their hard work and enterprising efforts led to substantial success. Great houses of business such as Straus, Morgenthau and Lehman were joined by others who became supporters of nascent Jewish social agencies.

Massive immigration of East European Jewry constituted the third wave of new settlers from 1880 to 1920. Statistically the Jewish population went from 3,000 to 15,000 between 1790 and 1840, from 15,000 to 250,000 between 1840 and 1880, and from 250,000 to 3,500,000 between 1880 and 1920. The computer banks of the Texas Seaport Museum in Galveston contain many of those immigration records.

With the beginning of the twentieth century, the Jewish community began to grow not only in number but also in achievement. At the same time that the early colonies were becoming established and the early Jewish settlers were finding homes in the United States, so were the Jews in Texas. As Texas entered into its struggle for independence from Mexico, numerous Jews were mentioned. Jacob Henry and Jacob Lyons were also patriotic citizen soldiers of the nascent republic who fought under General Tom Green, with whom Henry would serve as Surgeon General. An early Houston resident, Eugene Chimene, who came from France to Texas, also was a participant in the war with Mexico.

Some names have stood out more prominently than others in Texas history. Albert Moses Levy served as a Surgeon General to Sam Houston's forces and fought in the battle of San Jacinto. He settled in Matagorda County after the revolution and served on the first Texas Board of Medical Examiners. Herman Ehrenberg, Benjamin M.Mordecai, M.K.Moses and Edward I.Johnson of Cincinnati, were all participants in the battle of Goliad. Among the four, Johnson was killed along with 330 other prisoners by the Mexicans while Ehrenberg returned to Europe to later write of his experiences in Texas. Though Leon Dyer would gain a reputation as a collector of clippings and historical data, he gained early repute when he was assigned by Sam Houston to officially escort Santa Anna to Washington, D.C.,in November of 1836.

Three Jews gained much prominence in Texas in the early 1800's by virtue not of their military prowess, but their expertise in business, and by extension, their ability to attract newcomers to Texas. Henri Castro (1786-1865) served as minister to France from the Republic of Texas and was a major force in settling newcomers on the land west of San Antonio all the way to the Rio Grande River. Jacob de Cordova is said to have put Texas on the map of the world due to his extensive efforts at colonizing. De Cordova brought the Odd-Fellows to Texas, served as "Publicity Agent for an Empire," helped secure payment to Texas from the United States for lands delineated in the Compromise of 1850. The third of this special trio was Adolphus Sterne, who was the first Jew to serve in the Texas Legislature and brought Masonry to the State. In addition to fighting in the war for independence, Sterne also served in New Orleans outfitting new military groups to participate in the battle.

With the coming of independence, other members of the Jewish community assumed positions of responsibility in Texas. David S.Kaufman, of Nacogdoches, was twice Speaker of the Texas House and first U.S.Congressman for the new state, having already served President Anson Jones as Charge d'Affaires of Texas to the United States. In 1840, Simon Y.Weiss was appointed Deputy Collector of Customs by President Sam Houston. Weiss served until the end of the republic when he moved to Sabine Pass where he established a cotton trade moving bales on keelboats.

Texas was and is still an area of much ranching. Though only a few Jews were ever-true cattlemen, the names of some should clearly be noted. Mayer and Solomon Halff established ranches in Brewster County, Charles Weil registered the Cross Six brand for his ranch in Corpus Christi, Solomon Mayer registered the T Half Circle Ranch brand in San Angelo and A.Levytansky established his ranch in La Salle County in 1882. Providing the materials, which these early ranchers needed to facilitate their efforts, was the Kallison family, who still run one of the largest ranch and farm outfitter businesses.

As in many European countries, so too in Texas, Jews found their way into banking and merchandising. Among the bankers were Abraham Levi of Victoria in 1822, Daniel and Anton Oppenheimer in San Antonio whose families to this day run one of the oldest non-incorporated family banks, Fred F.Florence who brought Republic Bank of Dallas into prominence, Jules K.Hexter of Dallas and Hyman Pearlstone from Palestine, Texas, and founders of the First National Bank of Dallas. Among this group of pioneering financial risk takers there should also be listed Hyman Krupp whose persistence resulted in the west Texas oil fields and the wealth of the University of Texas system.

Clearly these are not the only Jews who early on were a part of settling Texas nor is this a complete history of the State. It is, however, fairly representative of the character of the early entrepreneurs and offers a background against which to view the establishment of Galveston and Temple B'nai Israel.

Galveston: The Island of Snakes

On the 6th of November, 1528, the population of Galveston Island expanded in a manner that permanently changed its character. To the Isla de Culebras or Island of Snakes, so named on early navigation charts because of its abundance of reptilians, the same island used by the Karankawa Indians for campsites, burial grounds, fishing and hunting, came Cabeza de Vaca and his Moor comrade, Estevancio. These Spanish explorers were looking for fame and fortune. The earliest name they gave to the Island was Malhaldo. This means "misfortune" and alludes either to the deprivations experienced by the Spanish or the diarrhea given to the Karankawas. Late the surveyor Hevia to honor Bernardo Galvez, the Spanish governor of Louisiana, gave the name "Galveston" to the bay area.

Records show that Jean Lafitte and his buccaneer followers took control of Galveston and used it as their base of operations until 1821. Though Galveston had few inhabitants, on October 17, 1825, the Island was designated a port of entry by the Congress of Mexico meeting in Mexico City. Though the Island itself did not play an active role in the war for Texas Independence which began in 1836, it was on Galveston Island that President David G.Burnet received the news of the Texan victory at San Jacinto on April 21, 1836.

Upon payment of the sum of $50,000.00, the Republic of Texas sold a league (four thousand four hundred and forty-four acres) and a labor (a lot of one hundred and seventy seven acres) of island land to one Michael B.Menard. This sale which took place on December 9, 1836, resulted in the formal establishment of the City of Galveston on the east end of Galveston Island.

In April of 1838, the Galveston City Company organized and elected a board of five directors. These directors were empowered to establish and sell lots for shareholders of the Company stock. Those first directors were M.B.Menard, President, Thomas F.McKinney, Samuel M.Williams, Mosely Baker and John K.Allen with Dr.Levi Jones as the General Agent of the Company.

In May 1838, Galveston County was established and one year later its boundaries were expanded. In the 1830's, Galveston was the site of the first post office in Texas, the first naval base, the first bakery and with the opening of the Morgan Line between Galveston and New Orleans, the first regular steamship service to Texas. Galveston became an incorporated city in

January, 1839, with a mayor-alderman form of government.

In all of the history of the Island, members of the Jewish community have figured prominently. In 1879, C. W. Hayes notes in his book *History of the Island and City of Galveston*, of the one hundred important people in Galveston's past, fourteen were Jewish.

It is likely that the first permanent Jewish settler on the Island was Joseph Osterman. Osterman was born in Amsterdam in 1779. After merchandising in Philadelphia and Baltimore where he married Rosana Dyer, he moved to Galveston in 1838. In April of that year when the first lots on the Island were sold, he bought on the corner of Market and Tremont where he built a two story house. After a very successful merchandising business, he then sold his business to his brother-in-law, Isadore Dyer. Mr. Dyer later provided his home for the first meetings of the Temple. Osterman's benevolence and concern for the city, which even included loaning money to the city, added all the more to the profound sorrow at his accidental death in 1861 due to the inadvertent discharge of a pistol undergoing repair.

Rosana Dyer Osterman, wife of Joseph and sister of Isadore, may be best remembered as the mother of the Jewish community. Through the beneficence of her last will and testament, among many other major charities, funds were provided for a synagogue and cemetery. From the death of her husband in 1861 until her own tragic death on the steam boat J.W.Carter, which burned on February 2, 1866, Rosana utilized her substantial inheritance to benefit those in need.

Completing this family portrait of early Jewry on Galveston Island is Isadore Dyer. He arrived in Galveston in 1840 and for two years clerked for Joseph Osterman. After establishing a very successful general merchandising business of his own. In 1865 Dyer was elected President of the Union and Marine Fire Insurance Company. Between 1854 and 1876, Dyer served as a city alderman, a county commissioner and treasurer of the Galveston Wharf and Cotton Press Company.

The first Jewish mayor of Galveston was Michael Seeligson. He was elected some hundred years before the first Jewish mayor of New York City. After arriving in Galveston in 1838, Seeligson became an alderman in 1841. After many years of service to the City, he retired to a ranch in Goliad. Henry Seeligson, Michael's son, established a successful banking house on the Island, H.Seeligson and Company, in 1874.

One of the earliest Jewish physicians to arrive in Galveston was Nicholas D.Labadie. Born in Windsor, Canada, he received his medical education in Missouri and arrived in Texas in 1830. Though never officially cited for his outstanding efforts, Labadie was a true Texan patriot. He served as a surgeon in Sam Houston's army and as Sam Houston' interpreter for Santa Anna. In

1838, Labadie settled in Galveston where he opened a drug store and functioned as one of the city's early physicians.

One last early Jewish settler of note was Sam Maas. He arrived in Galveston in 1844. A linguist of ability, he also served as interpreter for Sam Houston. Maas is best known for having married Isabella Offenbach, a popular German opera singer and the sister of Offenbach, a well known composer.

Over the next two decades Galveston witnessed the arrival of those Jews who would have the most lasting impact upon the Island. These later settlers were able to build upon the efforts of those who came before them. Clearly this select group represented the first of Galveston's creative entrepreneurs. In 1857, Moritz Kopperl landed in Galveston, having come from Moravia via New York and New Orleans. After some unsuccessful business activities with a Mr.Lipman before the Civil War, Kopperl established a substantial coffee importing business. In 1865, became president of the National Bank of Texas. In 1871, he became a city alderman and in 1876 a member of the Texas Legislature. Kopperl assumed the presidency of the Gulf, Colorado and Santa Fe Railroad Company in 1877, and brought the company to financial solvency. Kopperl is an example of the businessman who tried, failed, and tried again. Despite the business ups and downs, he persevered to become a major financial presence in the community.

The Civil War also changed the plans and early efforts of Leon Blum and Felix Halff. Blum, who came from Alsace, established his first business endeavors with Felix Halff, also from Alsace, in the southern parishes of Louisiana. After eighteen months of successful activity, they amicably dissolved the partnership. History would bring them together again as leading members of the Galveston Jewish community. Leon and his brother Alexander operated a successful staples operation that had to be moved to Matamoros, Mexico during the Civil War. In 1865, the brothers moved to Galveston and continued their efforts as wholesalers instead of retailers. Leon was the first merchant in Galveston to see the possibility of large, quick sales at smaller profits. Blum was an ardent believer in limited use of checks and his efforts in 1873 averted the type of financial crisis that was plaguing New York and New Orleans. In 1874 Leon became active in establishing the Peoples' Street Railway Company. In 1876 he was an active participant in the building of the Tremont Hotel and the first Cotton Exchange Building.

Felix Halff arrived in Galveston in 1865, but his business career began with his arrival from Alsace to Louisiana. Prior to the Civil War, first with Leon Blum and then later with his cousin, Meyer Halff, Felix was a successful pereginating merchant. Halff's main interest was cotton, which, of course, suffered greatly with the Union blockade of the Gulf Coast. He, too, found himself in Matamoros until 1865 and from there he carried on his business efforts. After the end of the Civil War, Halff returned to Galveston and established a wholesale dry goods business. In 1872, he formed a partnership with Albert Weis and opened an exclusive "gents' furnishing goods" business. An active member of the community, Halff became a city alderman in 1875.

In 1866, Julius Rosenfield came to Galveston after leaving the firm of Ratz and Barnes in New Orleans. A decorated Civil War hero, he had paid for the outfitting of an entire regiment in the Army of the Confederacy. After several years of business efforts on the Island, his wholesale notions business grew into the largest of its kind in Texas.

Following a most successful business career in New Orleans and Salt Lake City, M.Marx came to Galveston that he considered would become the commercial metropolis of the Southwest. Marx joined in partnership with Harris Kempner, and the two established a thriving business as wholesale grocers and dealers in foreign and domestic liquors. Morris Lasker, a young employee of Marx and Kempner, later broke away and built up his own grocery business. Utilizing his experience in management, Lasker went on to acquire large amounts of real estate and the Texas Star Flour Mills. His son, Albert, started his career in Galveston as a reporter for the Galveston News. After forty-four years of involvement with Lord and Thomas, and a fortune made in advertising, today Albert is considered the "father of modern advertising."

Harris Kempner arrived in Galveston in 1870, having come originally from Poland via Cold Springs, Texas. His successful endeavors with M.Marx in the wholesale grocery business led him into the fields of cotton, banking, insurance, real estate and sugar. The financial empire he built and based in Galveston was carried on by his descendent, Harris L.Kempner. In 1872, Harris married Eliza Seinsheimer and raised eleven children on the Island. Isaac Herbert (I.H.)Kempner took over the reins of the family enterprises upon his father`s death and later served as Mayor in 1917, president of the Galveston Cotton Exchange and commissioner of finance of the City. Henrietta Blum Kempner, his wife, served on the first P.T.A.in Galveston, was a member of the Galveston School Board and a member of the State Child Welfare Committee. Numerous other members of the Kempner family have been active in all areas of community activities.

Two years before Harris Kempner's arrival, Joseph Levy and his brother Ben established J.Levy and Brothers Livery and Undertaking. In addition to their activities in horses and coffins, the brothers were active in real estate, having built some of the early apartment houses on the Island. Prior to the 1900 storm, Joseph served as alderman in charge of fire and police, and as head of public works and supervised the laying of the first brick pavement in Galveston.

Isadore Lovenberg, originally from France, arrived in Galveston in 1873. For over thirty years, he served on the Galveston School Board, twelve of them as president. Robert I.Cohen arrived in Gavleston about four years after Lovenberg. He, too, like many others became involved in dry goods and opened his own store in 1889. In 1919, that store became Foley Brothers, which was later bought out by Federated Stores of Cincinnati.

In April, 1842, when the price of a ship passage to Houston was $5.00 and a trip to New Orleans was $25.00. During this same period of time Joseph Osterman's store had a one-third page ad in the newspaper. Two years later on February 24, 1844, two major ads were run in a Galveston newspaper by J.Osterman who specialized in "French, British and American Staple and Fancy Dry Goods." In May of that same year, ads appeared for J.Osterman, John Dyer (Leon's father) and H.Kaufman and Company. In that same newspaper, William Kennedy, the British consul, reported that an act of Parliament had been passed prohibiting British subjects or their vessels from engaging in the slave trade and that he was obligated to inspect all ships for illegal cargo. In 1848, ads also appeared for goods and services sold by N.D.Labadie, M.Seeligson and J.Dyer, along with articles by Jacob de Cordova, the Texas land and general agent.

In light of the numerous storms which Galveston records would have had to undergo, it is miraculous that any are extant. In 1850, the Federal census recorded that there were 3,469 single and family units l, 59 freed slaves, and 678 slaves. Among the Jews who were known to be in the City, the following were listed: Samuel Maas(30), Merchant, $3,000 real estate, Isabella(30), Maxwell(5), Julius(3), Mary(2), Alfred(1); Joseph Osterman(50), Merchant, $10,000 real estate, Rosanna(40), Hannah(25), Isabella(20), Mary(28); Isadore Dyer(35), Merchant, $4,500 real estate, Amelia(22), John(8), Emily(6), Leon(5), Rosana(4), Joe(2); M.Seeligson(52), Merchant, $7,000 real estate, Adaline(50), Jane(17), Adaline(16), Henrietta(10), Geo.(8); Is.R.Lyons(30), Bar Keep, Julia(25).

The 1860 census noted some changes and added some names: Samuel Maas, Merchant, owner of $50,000 real estate; Joseph Osterman, Gentleman, owner of $191,000 real estate; Isadore Dyer, Merchant, owner of $30,000 real estate; A.Blum(29), Merchant, owner of $3,000 real estate, b.France, Clara(19), Joseph(6); J.Blum(21), Clerk, b.France,Lilva(18).

In 1856, the first business directory lists the following: Dyer, I., Groceries, 22nd St., Home:I & 25th St.; Labadie, N., Drug Store, Market & 22nd; Levy, J., E & 18th St.; Labadies' Wharf, 27th St.; It also lists the following churches and ministers: Episcopal, Rev.B.Eaton; Catholic, Dr.J.M.Odin; Presbyterian, Mr.Mc Nair; Methodist, Rev.Seat; Baptist, Rev.Huckins, and Lutheran, Rev.Went.

The 1859-1860 Galveston Business Directory listed the following early Jews: Dyer, I., Groceries, 23rd-24th St., Home:I & 24th St.; Frank, J.W., Merchant, 21st & 23rd, D; Frank, L., Carpenter, 17th & 18th, B & C; Harby, I., U.S.N., C & 12th St.

Of special note are two entries in the Business Directory: Pg.118, Hebrew Benevolent Society, organized 1848, meets first Sunday of every month. President: S.E.Loeb; Vice President: J.Lieberman; Secretary: L.C.Michel; Treasurer: I.Dyer; Trustees: J.Rosenfield, W.Kory and L.Blum. Pg.116, Congregation B'nai Israel, organized 1868. President: J.W.Frank; Vice President: D.Wenar; Secretary: S.K.Labatt; Treasurer: M.Kopperl; Trustees: A.Kory, I.Fedder, and C.Kahn.

The following editorial footnote is found in the Galveston Daily News of 1866: "We are proud to chronicle that our Hebrew friends in this city are actively engaged in establishing and organizing Societies, Schools, etc. The School on Church Street, between Tremont and 24th Street, is now in a flourishing condition, and increasing daily in numbers. It is conducted by and under the charge of the able Professor, Mr.Alexander Rosenspitz. We also learn from some of the officers of the above Societies, that several lots, (situated on corner of Avenue I and 22nd Street), have been purchased for the erection of a Synagogue, the corner stone of which will soon be laid. We are glad to learn such news, for we can rest assured, whenever it will be completed, it will be an ornament to the city, that all may be proud of". Galveston Jewry had definitely taken hold on the island.

Jews have been active in the business, social, cultural and welfare fabric of the community from the beginning. In spite of this, not much is recorded about "Jewish" life of the Island until several decades had passed. The Hebrew Benevolent Society, which is the oldest Jewish organization in the State was certainly needed especially in light of the Yellow Fever epidemics. In any event, the establishment of a cemetery before a synagogue was typical of most new Jewish communities for over 1900 years.

The following article, which appeared in the November, 1866, edition of the Galveston Daily News, may have been one of the catalysts which led the Jews to begin organizing a permanent house of prayer.

"The Israelites are fast increasing in numbers in our city... We are all glad of this, because they make good, law-abiding citizens, and if the popular prejudice against them could be overcome — as it should be — traits of character which are admired and appreciated by every class, would be found quite common among them. But enough of this. Our intention is simply to call the attention of 'this chosen people' to this fact... Why don't the Israelites of our city build or rent a suitable hall for the purpose of excercising the peculiar rites of their religion? A few thousand dollars would be quite sufficient to erect a frame synagogue. If this cannot be done, some of the halls in our city would be doubtless obtained for the purpose... We hope we will not be misunderstood in noticing this subject. We believe emphatically in religiuos toleration, and as churches among the Christians are the means of improving the morals of any community, and are intended to benefit mankind generally, so we suppose the Jews will be improved by the erection of a synagogue. It would certainly bring before them the obligations of their religion, in the better observance of which they could not fail in being a better people."

Officers of the Temple

August 16, 1868

President	I.W.Frank
Vice President	I.H.Loeb
Secretary	S.K.Labatt

November 20, 1870

President	I.W.Frank
Vice President	Felix Halft
Secretary	S.K.Labatt
Treasurer	M.Kopperl
Trustees	L.C.Michael
	A.Korey
	Leon Blum

November 19, 1871

President	M.Kopperl
Vice President	Salomon Levy
Secretary	I.H.Loeb
Treasurer	I.Dyer
Trustees	F.Heidenheimer
	Sam Levy
	S.Halff
Shamas	Isaac Cohen

November 17, 1872

President	M.Kopperl
Vice President	A.Halff
Secretary	I.Lovenberg
Treasurer	I.Dyer
Trustees	S.Heidenheimer
	I.Blum
	A.Weiss
Shamas	Jacob Meyer

November 6, 1873

President	M.Kopperl
Vice President	J.W.Frank
Secretary	I.Lovenberg
Treasurer	I.Dyer
Trustees	S.Heidenheimer
	I.Blum
	H.Halff
School Trustees	J.Rosenfield
	D.Freeman
	I.Lovenberg

November 15, 1874

President	M.Kopperl
Vice President	F.Halff
Secretary	I.Lovenberg
Treasurer	I.Dyer
Trustees	I.Bernstein
	S.Heidenheimer
	L.Oppenheimer
School Trustees	I.Lovenberg
	D.Freeman
	J.Rosenfield

November 21, 1875

President	M.Kopperl

Vice President	F.Halff
Secretary	I.Lovenberg
Treasurer	I.Dyer
Trustees	Bernstein
	Michael
	Heidenheimer
School Trustees	Rosenfield
	Lovenberg
	J.Wrenk
Shamas	L.Cahn

November 18, 1876

President	M.Kopperl
Vice President	F.Halff
Secretary	I.Lovenberg
Treasurer	I.Dyer
Trustees	I.Bernstein
	L.C.Michael
	E.Friberg
School Trustees	A.Frankel
	J.Rosenfield
	K.I.Lovenberg

November 18, 1877

President	M.Kopperl
Vice President	F.Halff
Secretary	I.Lovenberg
Treasurer	I.Dyer
Trustees	I.Bernstein
	L.C.Michael
	J.M.Northman
School Trustees	A.Frankel
	J.Rosenfield
	I.Lovenberg
Hebrew School	M.Schram
	J.Wenk
A.Levy	

November 17, 1888

President	F.Halff
Vice President	L.C.Michael
Secretary	I.Holstein
Treasurer	I.Dyer
Trustees	M.Schram
	L.Lasker
	M.S.Mooney
School Trustees	A.Frenkel
	N.Freiberg
	J.Rosenfield
Hebrew School	M.Schram
	A.Levy
	I.Holstein

November 21, 1880

President	F.Halff
Vice President	L.C.Michael
Secretary	I.Holstein
Treasurer	I.Dyer
Trustees	M.Schram
	B.H.Jacobs
	M.Lasker
School Trustees	I.Lovenberg
	B.H.Jacobs
	C.B.Miller
Hebrew School	Alph.Dreyfus
	I.C.Levy

November 20, 1881

President	F.Halff
Vice President	L.C.Michael
Secretary	F.Schram
Treasurer	I.Dyer
Trustees	L.Weis
	M.Schram

School Trustees	M.Lasker
	C.B.Miller
	Mose Freiberg
	A.Frankel
Hebrew School	Northman
	B.H.Jacobs
Schamas	M.Mansberg

November 26, 1882

President	F.Halff
Vice President	L.C.Michael
Secretary	A.Cohen
Treasurer	I.Dyer
Trustees	L.Weis
	M.Lasker
	H.Flatto

November 18, 1883

President	F.Halff
Vice President	C.B.Miller
Secretary	A.Cohen
Treasurer	I.Dyer
Trustees	M.Lasker
	Leopold Weis
	H.Flatto
School Trustees	A.Frankel
	L.Kaufman
	J.R.Seligman
Schamas	M.Marsberg

November 16, 1884

President	F.Halff
Vice President	I.Heidenheimer
Secretary	A.Cohen
Treasurer	I.C.Levy
Trustees	L.Levin

86

	M.Marx
Schamas	J.Goldstein
	M.Marsberg

November 29, 1885

President	F.Halff
Vice President	Leo N.Levi
Secretary	A.Cohen
Treasurer	I.C.Levy
Trustees	M.Schram
	M.Marx
	I.Holstein

November 21, 1886

President	F.Halff
Vice President	Leo N.Levi
Secretary	A.Cohen
Treasurer	I.C.Levy
Trustees	Jac.Sonnenthiel
	I.Holstein
	M.Schram
School Trustees	A.Frankel
	Jake Wenth
	I.Lovenberg
Schamas	M.Marsberg

November 20, 1887

President	Leo N.Levi
Vice President	M.Schram
Secretary	I.Holstein
Treasurer	I.C.Levy
Trustees	J.Sonnenthiel
	J.Rosenfield
	N.Redlich
Schamas	M.Mansberg

November 18, 1888

President	Leo N.Levi
Vice President	M.Schram
Secretary	I.Holstein
Treasurer	I.C.Levy
Trustees	J.Sonnenthiel
	I.Redlich
	J.Rosenfield
School Trustees	J.Rosenfield
	Holstein
	J.Went
Schamas	M.Mansberg

November 17, 1889

President	Leo N.Levi
Vice President	M.Schram
Secretary	I.Holstein
Treasurer	J.Rosenfield
	N.Redlich
	I.Frenkel
School Trustees	D.Schwarz
	Hy Freiberg
	B.A.Isaacs
Schamas	M.Mansberg

November 15, 1891

President	Leo N.Levi
Vice President	M.Schram
Secretary	I.Holstein
Treasurer	J.Sonnenthiel
Trustees	J.Rosenfield
	A.Frenkel
	J.Wenk
School Trustees	D.Schwartz
	A.Isaacs
	Hy Frieberg
Schamas	M.Mansberg

November 20, 1892

President	Leo N.Levi
Vice President	M.Schram
Secretary	I.Holstein
Treasurer	J.Sonnenthiel
Trustees	J.Wenk
	J. Weinberger
	M.Freiberg
School Trustees	D.Schwarz
	B.Isaacs
	Hy Freiberg

November 18, 1894

President	Leo N.Levi
Vice President	M.Schram
Secretary	Henry Frieberg, Jr.
Treasurer	J.Sonnenthiel
Trustees	I.Holstein
	C.Schwarz
	M.Maas
SchoolTrustee	Schwarz
	Henry Frieberg
	B.A.Isaacs
Schamas	M.Marsberg

November 19, 1894

Same Officers

November 17, 1895

President	Leo N.Levi
Vice President	M.Schram
Secretary	I.Holstein
Treasurer	J.Sonnenthiel
Trustees	D.Schwarz
	M.Maas
	Hy Freiberg

89

School Trustees	D.Schwarz
	B.A.Isaacs
	Hy Freiberg
Schamas	M.Marsberg

November 15, 1896

Same Officers

November 21, 1897

Same Officers

November 20, 1898

Same Officers

August 17, 1899

Leo N.Levi resigned as President to move to New York. He wrote, "and now I sorrowfully set to paper my farewell to all members of our association. May He, to whose glory we organized, never avert His face from any of them."

May 20, 1900

Minutes illegible

November 16, 1902

President	Robert I.Cohen
Vice President	J.L.Ullmann
Secretary	H.B.Mayer
Treasurer	Max Maas
Trustees	J.S.Miller
	J.Singer
	S.Schornstein
School Trustees	B.A.Isaacs
	S.W.Levy
	J.Bonart
Schamas	M.Mansberg

November 22, 1903

Same Officers

May 15, 1904

Same Officers

November 16, 1905

Same Officers

November 18, 1906

President	Robert I.Cohen
Vice President	J.L.Ullmann
Secretary	H.B.Mayer
Treasurer	J.S.Miller
Trustees	J.Singer
	S.Schornstein
	Morris Stein
School Trustees	J.Bonart
	Max Levy
	B.Isaacs

November 17, 1907

Same Officers

November, 1908

Same Officers

November, 1909

Same Officers

November, 1910

Same Officers

June 14, 1911

Same Officers

March 1, 1914

President	Robert I.Cohen
Vice President	J.L.Ullman
Secretary	Louis Gernsbacher
Treasurer	Jos.Bonart
Trustees	S.Schornstein
	MorrisStein
	H.B.Meyer
School Trustees	B.Isaacs
	Max Levy
	Sam Shlansky
Schamas	Sylvan Miller

February 13, 1916

President	Robert I.Cohen
Vice President	I.Lovenberg
Secretary	Louis Gernsbacher
Treasurer	Jos.Bonart
Trustees	D.W.Kempner
	Edward Lasker
	H.B.Meyer
School Trustees	B.A.Isaacs
	Max Levy
	Sam Schlansky
Schamas	Sylvan Miller

January 13, 1918

President	Robert I.Cohen
Vice President	Aaron Blum
Secretary	S.Schlansky
Treasurer	J.Bonart
Trustees	D.W.Kempner
	Edward Lasker
	H.B.Meyer
School Trustees	B.A.Isaacs
	Max Levy

| | Sam Schlansky |
| Schamas | A.Rosenfield |

February 23, 1919

Same Officers

January 11, 1920

Same Officers except
Secretary   D.C.Himler

February 5, 1922

President	Robert I.Cohen
Vice President	Aaron Blum
Secretary	Emil Kahn
Treasurer	Jos.Bonart
Trustees	Hermann Nussbaum
	Abe Blum
	G.H.Aronsfeld
School Trustees	B.A.Isaacs
	Hyman Block
	Sol Levy
Schamas	August Rosenfield

January 13, 1924

Same Officers	
Trustees	G.H.Aronsfeld
	JulesBlock
	AdrianLevy
	Mrs.I.H.Kempner
	Mrs.Max Levy

January 11, 1925

President	Robert I.Cohen
1st Vice President	John Neethe
2nd Vice President	Herman Nussbaum

Secretary	Emil Kahn
Treasurer	Lee Kempner
Trustees	G.H.Aronsfeld
	Jules Block
	Adrian Levy
	Mrs.I.H.Kempner
	Mrs.Max Levy
School Trustees	B.A.Isaacs
	Hyman Block
	Sol Levy
Schamas	August Rosenfield

January 23, 1927

President	Robert I.Cohen
lst Vice President	John Neethe
2nd Vice President	H.Nussbaum
Secretary	Emil Kahn
Treasurer	R.Lee Kempner
Trustees	Jules Block
	Mrs.I.H.Kempner
	Adrian Levy
	G.H.Aronsfeld
	Mrs.Max Levy
School Trustees	B.A.Isaacs
	S.W.Levy
	H.S.Block
Schamas	A.M.Rosenfield

January 21, 1929

Same Officers except	
Secretary	M.Heidenheimer

January 14, 1930

Same Officers except	
1st V.P.	Adrian Levy

94

January 29, 1931

President	Robert I.Cohen
lst Vice President	Adrian Levy
2nd Vice President	S.S.Kay
Secretary	Mose Heidenheimer
Treasurer	Lee Kempner
Trustees	John Neethe
	Yetta Kahn
	H.H.Levy
	Jules Block
	Mrs.I.H.Kempner
	G.H.Aronsfeld
	Mrs.Max Levy

March 9, 1932

Same Officers except

Trustee	A.Oshman

January 26, 1933

Same Officers

December 31, 1934

Same Officers except
Secretary Joseph Levy

March 12, 1935

President	I.H.Kempner
lst Vice President	Adrian Levy
2nd Vice President	S.S.Kay
Secretary	Joseph Levy
Treasurer	Hyman Block
Trustees	J.F.Seinsheimer
	M.Bodansky
	Morris Burka
	Mrs.Yetta Kahn

95

96

January 19, 1938

President	Adrian Levy, Sr.
1st Vice President	J.F.Seinsheimer
2nd Vice President	Leopold Schornstein
Secretary	S.S.Kay
Treasurer	Hyman Block
Trustees	Gladys Blum
	Marvin Kahn
	David Nathan
	A.Oshman,
	Bernard Kauffman
	Ethel Nierman
	Lee Kempner
	John Frenkel
School Trustees	JackIsaacs
	D.Stein
	M.Bodansky
	H.Levy

January 17, 1939

President	Meyer Bodansky
1st Vice President	J.F.Seinsheimer
2nd Vice President	Leopold Schornstein
Secretary	S.S.Kay
Treasurer	Hyman Block
Trustees	Gladys Blum
	I.M.Herz
	Bernard Kaufman
	Lee Kempner
	Al Levine
	Marion Levy
	W.Zinn
	A.Oshman
	S.B.Shapiro
	Morris Melcer
	Dave Nathan

97

School Trustees	Nettie Schornstein A.Bernheim Jack Isaacs Marvin Kahn, Joseph Nierman H.H.Levy, Jr.

February 14, 1940

Same Officers

January 28, 1941

Same Officers except
lst VP	S.S.Kay

January 14, 1942

President	S.S.Kay
lst Vice President	L.A.Schornstein
2nd Vice President	Dave Nathan
Secretary	M.S.Isaacs
Treasurer	B.L.Kauffman
Trustees	Staggered Terms

3 year	2 year	1 year
I.E.Burka	Harris Kempner	M. Baum
I.M.Herz	R.I.Cohen	ALLevine
M.D.Kahn	A.Oshman	H.S.Block
Sol Levy	H.Swiff	J.Swiff
S.Shapiro	Mrs.Sam Zinn	
School Trustees	J.Isaacs	
	J.Nierman	
	H.Levy	
	Ben Levy	

January 7, 1943

President	S.S.Kay
lst Vice President	Dave Nathan
2nd Vice President	I.E.Burka

98

Secretary	M.S.Isaacs
Treasurer	B.L.Kauffman
Trustess—3 yr.	R.L.Kempner
	L.A.Schornstein
	Herbert Garon
	H.H.Levy, Jr.

January 12, 1944

President	S.S.Kay
lst Vice President	Dave Nathan
2nd Vice President	I.E.Burka
Secretary	M.S.Isaacs
Treasurer	I.M.Herz
Trustees—3 yr.	Henry Block
	Harry Davidson
	Joe Levy
	D.M.Goldhirsh
School Trustees	J.Isaacs
	Ethel Nierman
	Elanor Bodansky
	Regina Seidl
	Pauline Zinn

January 16, 1946

President	Dave Nathan
lst Vice President	H.H.Levy
2nd Vice President	I.E.Burka
Secretary	M.S.Isaacs
Treasurer	I.M.Herz
Trustees	

3 year	2 year	1 year
B.L.Kauffman	Julian Levy	H. Block
Bill Levin	B.Demoratsky	H.Davidson
M.Messinger	Adam Levy	D.Goldhirsh
Sol Levy	Ben Levy	Joe Levy
School Trustees	Jack Isaacs	

99

Schamas

Ethel Nierman
Joe Isenberg

January 15, 1947

President	Dave Nathan	
lst Vice President	I.E.Burka	
2nd Vice President	Bernard Kauffman	
Secretary	I.M.Herz	
Treasurer	Adam Levy	
Trustees		

3 years	2 year	1 year
Leon Blum	Bill Levin	B.Demoratsky
L.Gernsbacher	Sol Levy	Mat Colby
Mrs.I.H.Kempner	Mike Mesinger	Ben Levy
Leo.Schornstein	Frank Nussbaum	Julian Levy

January 18, 1949

President	B.L.Kauffman
lst Vice President	S.B.Shapiro
2nd Vice President	Lew Harris
Secretary	A.M.Kottwitz
Treasurer	D.M.Goldhirsh

January 31, 1950

President	S.B.Shapiro
lst Vice President	Adrian Levy, Jr.
2nd Vice President	L.A.Schornstein
Secretary	A.S.Kottwitz
Treasurer	Ben Levy
Trustees—3 yrs.	H.Levy, Jr
	Adam Levy
	D.Goldhirsh
	Bill Levin
	Robert Cohen, III

January 25, 1954

President	Adrian Levy, Jr.
1st Vice President	L.A.Schornstein
2nd Vice President	Lewis Harris
Secretary	A.S.Kottwitz
Treasurer	O.L.Selig

January 10, 1956

President	Bill Levin
1st Vice President	Lewis Harris
2nd Vice President	Peter Kamin
Secretary	B.Demoratsky
Treasurer	Paul Lipnick

May 27, 1959

President	Lewis Harris
1st Vice President	Morris Pollard
2nd Vice President	Oury Selig
Secretary	Ben Patch
Treasurer	Joe Schlansky

April 10, 1961

President	Lewis Harris
1st Vice President	Morris Pollard
2nd Vice President	Howard Krantz
Secretary	Eli Perry
Treasurer	Aaron Littmann

March 11, 1963

President	Arthur Alpert
1st Vice President	Joe Levy
2nd Vice President	Ben Nathan
Secretary	Paul May
Treasurer	Aaron Littmann

March 9, 1964

President	Joseph Levy
1st Vice President	Ben Klein
2nd Vice President	Ben Nathan
Secretary	Paul May
Treasurer	Aaron Littmann

April 11, 1966

President	Ben Klein
1st Vice President	Ben Levy
2nd Vice President	Ben Nathan
Secretary	Sid Kay
Treasurer	Aaron Littmann

April 8, 1968

President	Ben Nathan
1st Vice President	Neil Nathan
2nd Vice President	Sid Kay
Secretary	Evelyn Krantz
Treasurer	Aaron Littmann

April 14, 1969

President	Neil Nathan
1st Vice President	Sid Kay
2nd Vice President	Don Sussan
Secretary	Evelyn Krantz
Treasurer	Aaron Littmann

April 10, 1972

President	Sid Kay
1st Vice President	Irwin M. Herz, Jr.
2nd Vice President	Evelyn Krantz
Secretary	Doris Labowitz
Treasurer	Aaron Littmann

April 8, 1974

President	Ben Levy
1st Vice President	Irwin M. Herz, Jr.
2nd Vice President	Evelyn Krantz
Secretary	Doris Gill
Treasurer	Aaron Littmann

April 21, 1975

President	Irwin M. Herz, Jr.
1st Vice President	Evelyn Krantz
2nd Vice President	Tim Thompson
Secretary	Gene Hornstein
Treasurer	Aaron Littmann

May 10, 1978

President	Evelyn Krantz
1st Vice President	Tim Thompson
2nd Vice President	Jack Alperin
Secretary	Ann Masel
Treasurer	Aaron Littmann

May 13, 1981

President	Tim Thompson
1st Vice President	Jack Alperin
2nd Vice President	Grace Jameson
Secretary	Marc Weiss
Treasurer	Aaron Littmann

May 12, 1982

President	Tim Thompson
1st Vice President	Grace Jameson
2nd Vice President	Marilyn Schwartz
Secretary	Danny Gold
Treasurer	Aaron Littmann

May 12, 1983

President	Grace Jameson
1st Vice President	Gerald Cohen
2nd Vice President	Michael Warren
Secretary	Barbara Crews
Treasurer	Aaron Littmann

May 14, 1985

President	Michael Warren
1st Vice President	Robert Rose
2nd Vice President	Ann Masel
Secretary	Marilyn Hershman
Treasurer	Aaron Littmann

May 14, 1988

President	Robert Rose
1st Vice President	David Jameson
2nd Vice President	Ann Masel
Secretary	Marilyn Hershman
Treasurer	Aaron Littmann

May 14, 1989

President	David Jameson
1st Vice President	Marc Shabot
2nd Vice President	Brentg Masel
Secretary	David Davis
Treasurer	Aaron Littmann
Honorary President	Aaron Littmann

May 12, 1992

President	Marc Shabot
1st Vice President	Brent Masel
2nd Vice President	Barbara Jane (B.J.) Herz
Secretary	Cindy Stein
Treasurer	Marshall Stein

May 12, 1996

President	Brent Masel
1st Vice President	Barbara Jane (B.J.) Herz
2nd Vice President	Randy Goldblum
Secretary	Karen Kronenberg
	Ellen Goldhirsh
Treasurer	Marshall Stein

May 12, 1998

President	Barbara Jane (B.J.) Herz
1st Vice President	Randy Goldblum
2nd Vice President	Robert Goldhirsh
Secretary	Carla Brandon
Treasurer	Marshall Stein

May 12, 2000

President	Randy Goldblum
1st Vice President	Robert Goldhirsh
2nd Vice President	Nat Shapiro
Secretary	Carla Brandon
Treasurer	Marshall Stein

May 12, 2002

President	Robert Goldhirsh
1st Vice President	Nat Shapiro
2nd Vice President	Barbara Crews
Secretary	Carla Brandon
Treasurer	Marshall Stein

Members of Temple B'nai Israel

A fairly complete list of all members of Temple B'nai Israel appears in the minutes of the Congregation. The following information comes from those minutes and other documents found in the files of the Temple. The names appear in the chronological order they are found in the records and only by male names. When the same date applies in sequence to several names, only one date is noted.

I.W.Frank,	08-16-1868
Leon Blum	
I.Dyer	
S.E.Loeb,	honorary member
M.Kopperl	
S.K.Labatt	
Ben C.Levy	
I.Wenk	
M.N.Lesive	
M.A.King,	08-01-1869
M.B.King	
Sylvain Levy	
I.H.Loeb	
M.Strauss	

J.Liberman
M.Arnold
A.Loeb
Theo Irving
M.Metzger
M.Arnold
Sylvan Blum
Henry Blum
Joseph Blum,   09-11-1869
Jos.Blum, Jr.
I Bernstein,   09-11-1869
I.Blumenkrone
Lanis Block
Louis Feinberg
Isadore Feist
I.Holstein
L.C.Michael
M.Miguel
P.H.Monis
L.Oppenheimer
J.Rosenfield
Julius Sonnentheil
Henry Wenar
I.Reinasier
Leon Theophile
Henry Cerf
F.Lidenthal
H.Flatto,   10-10-1869
A.Kory
H.James
I.Levy
I.Block,   11-14-1869
W.Dreyfus
J.Fedder,   11-27-1869
A.Cohen
I.Jalonick,   01-12-1870
I.Rosenbaum,   04-10-1870

Meyer Schram	
Henry Weil	
L.Moos	
M.Marx	
L.Gross	
Nathan Arnold	
H.G.Weil	
M.H.Schwartz	
Max Maas,	04-25-1870
Joseph Levy,	04-26-1870
S.Heidenheimer,	05-15-1870
Simon Mayer,	05-25-1870
John Levy	
M.Hyman,	06-19-1870
A.Heidenheimer	
Frankel Lyons	
S.Levy	
M.Cohen,	08-14-1870
Charles Blum	
D.Freeman,	09-18-1870
Sam Levy	
F.Halff,	09-21-1870
Ed Kauffman	
Bernard Levy,	11-23-1870
Sylvan Lyons	
A.Lyons	
Albert Weis,	01-29-1871
Leon Weis	
G.Feist	
Israel Blum,	02-21-1871
R.Carrow,	03-05-1871
G.Lewis	

At this point in the minutes, Membership Committee reports were no longer included, but the vote on new members was included.

Alphonse Levy,	05-29-1871
H.I.Labatt,	08-20-1871
Jacob Davis,	09-03-1871
I.Stein	
I.Cahn	
I.Schornstein	
I.Lovenberg	
I.Sonnentheil, Jr.	
G.Kauffman	
Alex Ortlieb	
I.L.Hirsh	
Clarence Barnett	
I.Gottchalk	
Ben Blum	
H.Kempner	
N.Back	
E.G.Weil	
H.Hauser	
H.Metzger	
I.Wrenk	
H.Vogel	
James Schuller	
H.Prince	
E.Cahn	
I.Schlesinger	11-19-1871
H.J.Harby	
C.E.Saloman,	01-14-1872
Hermann Hirsh,	02-01-1872
Louis Heller,	02-18-1872
Joseph Dannenbaum	
A.Frankel,	04-14-1872
C.Heidenheimer,	05-19-1872
I.Billing,	05-19-1872
A.Potowsky,	05-19-1872
L.Lion	
M.Ostricher	
B.Oberstein,	10-31-1873

G.Pessils,	01-25-1874
S.Mooney	
H.Wurtzberger	
E.Bauman,	03-08-1874
H.W.Weis	
I.Heidenheimer,	05-14-1874
M.Woolf,	08-09-1874
H.H.Jacobs,	08-30-1874
M.J.Jacobs	
Joe Seinsheimer	
M.Samuel	
S.Berwin	
A.Levy	
M.Burgower,	09-27-1874
H.Wayenin	
W.Hirsch	
H.Kempner,	11-05-1874
Charles Miller,	05-23-1874
I.Locha,	06-12-1875
D.Stern,	09-05-1875
L.Eldridge	
D.M.Ehrlich,	10-31-1875
Julius Cahn	
E.Keoffer	
A.S.Wolff,	11-21-1875
J.M.Northman	
M.Lasker,	04-16-1876
N.Redlich,	08-20-1876
J.Bernheim	
E.Friberg,	08-20-1876
F.W.Beckhardt,	08-27-1876
A.Ortlieb,	09-09-1876
M.Freiberg	
L.Kaufman	
L.Jacobs,	09-26-1876
Ben Levy,	03-04-1877
W.H.Lowenstein,	09-23-1877

M.Samuels,	03-17-1878
H.Schwartz,	04-29-1878
H.Flatto	
J.D.Glicksman	
J.Poisnansky	
S.Leavesk	
J.Goldstein	
P.Goldstein	
I.Fedder,	04-29-1878
B.H.Jacobs	
Charles I.Kay,	08-18-1878
L.Klopman,	02-02-1879
L.Fellman,	04-06-1879
E.Elias	
Aaron Dreyfus,	05-04-1879
M.Rosenbaum	
Isaac Cohen,	07-04-1880
L.Wollstein,	04-24-1881
I.Bernstein	
J.R.Seligman,	05-15-1881
H.Kauffman,	08-21-1881
A.Cohen	
Jos.A.Blum,	09-01-1881
Jake Cohen	
M.D.Glicksman	
N.Grumbach	
M.E.Lazarus	
M.M.Levy	
Jacob Kahn	
L.Marx	
I.B.Mayer	
M.Rosenfield	
S.J.Sampson	
F.Schramm	
Achille Meyer	
Sol Kauffman,	09-19-1881
M.Weinberger,	11-20-1881

Henry Lord,	11-11-1882
Emanuel Longini	
S.Jacobs	
Robert I.Cohen,	03-04-1882
M.Grumbach,	04-06-1882
H.Freeberg	
J.Blum,	05-09-1882
J.Davis	
J.S.Miller	
R.E.Seligman	
F.Milheiser,	09-03-1882
J.W.Wenk,	10-21-1882
D.Bloch	
Simon Kaufman,	11-26-1882
E.S.Levy	
H.Sander	
M.Kahn,	04-15-1883
M.Herz	
Robert Weis,	06-03-1883
M.Ullman,	07-01-1883
Louis Gabert,	10-07-1883
P.Levine,	10-07-1883
Edward Cohn,	11-04-1883
M.E.Tansick,	02-03-1884
Leo.Zander	
M.M.Levy	
Moses Freiberg	
Jake Davis	
Jake Stern,	03-16-1884
I.Dopres,	09-14-1884
Louis Marx	
D.Schwartz	
B.Blum	
Alex Orslich,	09-28-1884
H.Freiberg, Jr.,	02-01-1885
C.Lowenstein,	03-22-1885
L.Baum,	05-17-1885

M.Brock
D.Freeman
M.Freyberg
L.Goodman
L.Harris
M.Gross
F.Kastan
Gus Levy
L.W.Landsberg
Joe Levy
Ben Levy
J.Lieberman
Z.Posnainsky
M.Schram
Jac.Weinberger
A.M.Rosenfield
R.Brach
Nathan Arnold
Louis Schlesinger
M.Schloss
B.A.Isaacs
Ed.Kauffman
Ben Blum
M.Seligman
H.Grumbach,   11-12-1885
Leo N.Levi
Leopold Weis
E.Mayer
P.Levine,   09-19-1886
H.Krupper
L.Heller
Ben Levy,   11-21-1886
M.Solomon,   12-05-1886
A.Davis
M.Rice,   11-06-1887
A.Rosenwald
J.Goldstein

A.Blum
Gus Levy,   03-18-1888
Jake Cohn
S.Gernsbacher,   05-01-1888
E.E.Ephraim,   07-23-1888
E.Samuels,   08-18-1888
S.Rosenfield
J.E.Wolf,   01-07-1889
C.M.Shayer,   03-24-1889
Jos.Blum,   04-25-1889
Sol Kauffman,   04-27-1889
J.Singer,   05-16-1889
Joe A.Blum,   08-18-1889
G.Posnainsky,   09-01-1889
J.E.Ikelheimer,   10-13-1889
Marks Kory
B.F.Castrow
M.Brock
L.Bloch
I.W.Greenwall,   10-27-1889
Morris Sass,   11-17-1889
Max Herz
A.Waag,   12-29-1889
A.M.Rosenfield,   04-03-1890
Joseph Levy,   08-31-1890
N.N.Jacob,   09-01-1890
Louis Goldschmidt,   09-22-1890
Julius Cahn
L.Heller,   11-09-1890
Baruch Levy
A.Rosenwald,   01-01-1891
Able Blum
L.Ullmann
M.C.Michael,   02-15-1891
B.Baer
S.J.Rosenfield
Max Zander

I.Goldstein	
Aron Drey,	03-01-1891
Sol Jacobs,	05-17-1891
R.J.Crohn	
Mrs.C.Hyman	
Max Stiefel,	08-16-1891
D.Borchard,	09-20-1891
M.E.Tausick	
Leonard Mueller	
E.Saloman,	10-07-1891
Louis Sinsheimer,	10-07-1891
Louis Levy	
Gab.Block,	11-14-1891
Gus Feist	
Julius Adam,	11-20-1891
B.Rauch,	11-27-1891
Emil Kahan,	12-04-1891
Leopold Block,	12-10-1891
Achille Meyer	
E.Ephraim,	04-01-1892
F.Freund,	11-20-1892
E.Bonart	
Sol Kaufman	
S.Schornstein	
H.L.Stern	
M.Kahn,	12-01-1892
I.E.Ikelheimer,	03-19-1893
Adolphe Good,	04-18-1893
A.Rosenwald,	05-22-1893
Sam H.Frenkel	
Sam Zander	
A.Heidenheimber,	06-01-1893
A.Chimene,	07-01-1893
Joe Blum,	08-01-1893
Leon Lewis	
Joe Bonard	
J.Schornstein	

Ike Meyer,	08-29-1893
G.Baer,	09-02-1893
Geo.Isaacs,	09-19-1893
Alfred Levi,	01-28-1894
D.Rouh,	03-11-1894
Isaac Markowitz,	05-01-1894
S.Levor,	04-01-1894
F.A.Gutman	
Ben Bonart	
M.L.Malwinsky,	06-23-1894
Wolf Wenk,	09-16-1894
Robert Weis	
Raoul Dreyfus	
Jules Block	
Nah.N.Jacobs,	10-04-1894
Harry Simon	
Max Rice	
James Kray	
Louis Marx	
Gus Levy	
Nettie Leives,	11-18-1894
Isaac Kempner,	12-09-1894
Morris Stern	
H.Meyer,	12-09-1894
Charles Blum	
L.Weiss	
M.Rosenberger	
Emile Block	
G.G.Levy,	01-01-1895
G.G.Dreyfus	
J.Spiro,	07-01-1895
Sam Seavil,	08-25-1895
Hermann Meyer	
Mrs.R.Schayer,	09-15-1895
Edw.Heishfield	
Morris Wansker	
M.S.Riglander	

M.M.Goldman	
M.N.Bleich,	02-02-1896
J.Singer,	08-09-1896
W.B.Nachman,	10-04-1896
Paul Oettinger	
Mrs.P.Stern	
Julius Forcheimer	
H.Y.Levine	
Mrs.M.Kory,	02-14-1897
Max Levy	
A.W.Samuels	
H.A.Rudnick,	05-02-1897
A.Hagenbacher	
B.Beekman	
M.Mansberg	
Sam Herman	
H.J.Labatt	
Hy.Cook	
Ben Kahn,	11-21-1897
Sam W.Black,	04-17-1898
Simon Louis	
Leo Posner,	08-08-1898
Sam J.Rosenfield,	11-20-1898
Jack A.Isaacs,	12-12-1898
Hiram Cohen,	04-24-1899
H.H.Cohen	
Emil Cohn	
Charles Davis	
Gus.Dreyfus	
A.Flatto	
A.M.Franks	
Charles Frenkel	
Dave Heidenheimer	
W.B.Labatt	
Harry H.Levy	
G.W.Levy	
David Marx,	04-24-1899

Maurice Meyers
H.H.Morris
R.S.Oppenheimer
Chas.Posnainsky
D.Sachs
Max Schnitzer
D.W.Schramm
Dan Sonnentheil
C.L.Weis
Sol Harris
H.Hergman
Morris Block
Sol Bromberg
Louis H.Fellman
Max Grumbach
I.Hauser
H.H.Jacob
Abe Kaufman
M.Kulewic
Sam Lazarus
I.Markowitz
J.Markowitz
M.C.Michael
Sam Raphel
M.D.Glicksman
R.C.Pollock
M.Rosenberg
Mrs.Julie Adams,   08-20-1899
Fred Milheiser
Isidore Predecki
Sam Levine,   09-29-1899
A.Gugenheim
B.B.Schram,   11-01-1899
Sam Migel,   01-01-1900
Gust.Block,   02-01-1900
M.Burgower,   04-22-1900
H.Blankfield

Miss.B.Doppelmeyer
Jacob Falk,   05-01-1900
Sol Bromberg,   03-03-1901
Leopold Weis
G.L.Weis
Louis Seinsheimer
Henry Moritz
Dan Kempner
Joe Kauffman
Abe Kauffman
L.Kaminski
Jacob Falk,
Mrs.A.Davis,   03-03-1901
P.Levine,   05-19-1901
Sam Zander,   09-08-1901
Sylvain Miller,   11-17-1901
Isaac Lovenberg
F.A.Gutman,   03-16-1902
David Schram
Mrs.Lyman Rosenfield
M.Block,   09-21-1902
E.Mayer
S.H.Frenkel
Jacob Meyer
Sol Mehrbach
H.J.Meyer
J.Weisbert
Sam Lovenberg
Leon G.Levy,   03-15-1903
J.Littman
Jonas Weinberger, 05-05-1903
Mrs.A.Waag
Sol Bromberg,   02-21-1904
Aaron Levy,   03-01-1904
Sol Bromberg,   04-01-1904
Dave Heidenheimer
Dan Kahn

Joseph Seaman,	07-01-1904
Lee Kempner	
Mrs.Anna Lord,	09-01-1904
Louis Himelfarb,	10-01-1904
Mose Heidenheimer	
Harry Weiss,	11-01-1904
H.Buchwald	
E.Hyman,	01-01-1905
Dan Robinson	
F.G.Weis,	11-29-1904
Sol Davis	
Edward Lasker,	01-01-1905
M.Schwartz,	01-01-1905
Mrs.Alphonse Levy,	03-12-1905
Sam Fridner,	05-01-1905
Michael Tack	
Sam J.Levy,	06-01-1905
A.Silvers	
D.Weinberger	
T.Sakowitz,	10-01-1905
Phil Limm	
Dave Schram	
Jake Ross	
T.D.Meyer	
Sam Miller	
Julius Maas,	11-01-1905
Max Maas, Jr.	
L.Kaminski,	02-01-1906
Leon Mossbacher,	03-01-1906
I.Hauser	
Sidney Hertz,	04-01-1906
B.Alderman,	05-01-1906
D.Weinberger	
I.J.Schmitt	
Geo.J.Hochstein,	06-01-1906
Mose Holland	
G.H.Aronfeld,	09-01-1906

H.A.Philipson	
Mrs.P.Stein	
Sam Raphael	
A.M.Franks	
Simon Sakowitz	
Joe Weisberg	
Perry Adler	
E.J.Wulfe	
Mrs.L.H.Fritzel	
Geo.Cohen,	10-01-1906
Nathan Maas,	11-01-1906
L.Fadin,	02-01-1907
Carl Feist	
L.Silberman	
J.Ullmann	
Irwing Ullmann	
Stanley Kempner,	03-01-1907
Joseph Lippmann	
J.Seinsheimer,	04-01-1907
H.L.Walters,	09-01-1907
M.D.Waldman	
Ben Sass	
J.Weisberg,	10-01-1907
Sol Davis,	11-01-1907
A.Buchwald,	12-01-1907
C.Brand,	12-01-1907
Geo.Bowsky,	02-01-1908
Sam Schlansky,	04-01-1908
S.Cohn,	06-01-1908
Lawrence Samuels,	09-01-1908
Sol Kauffman	
J.M.Wolff,	10-01-1908
B.A.Levine	
C.M.Wolfe	
Isadore Welch	
Chas.Davis,	11-01-1908
D.Woolf,	02-01-1909

Joe Kauffman,	03-01-1909
L.Sheikowitz	
Sol Levy,	09-01-1909
Sol Blum	
Ike Posner	
Jack Levy,	02-01-1910
R.I.Cohen, Jr.	04-01-1910
L.Kerpel	
Lucien H.Levy	
Mrs.L.Bernheim	
James Levine,	05-01-1910
N.Braun,	06-01-1910
Jake O'Donnell	
Chas.Kapner	07-01-1910
M.Rosenblatt,	10-01-1910
Adolph Mayer	
Emil Kahn	
H.Bell	
J.Miner	
H.Bernheimer,	02-11-1911
Emil Block,	10-11-1911
Joseph Cohen,	08-24-1911
H.Browner,	09-09-1911
Sig Block,	09-22-1911
Chas.Newding,	10-30-1911
Alfred Heidenheimer,	10-01-1912
Louis Tobler,	09-04-1912
S.Samuels,	09-16-1912
I.Samuels	
Chas.Littman	
Landman	
B.Adler	
M.Flatto	
J.Greenblatt	
J.Weinberger	
Sam Zinn,	02-12-1913
Mrs.Bernnie Sproule	

G.Leiberman,	04-08-1913
Dwight Lieb,	05-01-1913
Sam Fisher,	06-01-1913
Ned Lerner	
Perry Adler,	09-12-1913
I.Hauser,	10-01-1913
I.Gerbert	
Max Block	
M.Klein	
H.Norris	
Carl Unger	
Mrs.M.Rice	
Morris Melcer,	11-10-1913
Emil Kahn	
V.H.Unger,	03-01-1914
H.B.Unger	
J.Levis,	04-01-1914
D.S.Picard	
M.Epstein,	05-01-1914
H.Annstein	
Sol Fridner,	09-01-1914
M.S.Isaacs	
I.Mose	
J.S.Levy	
Morris Sass	
Mrs.P.Stein	
S.J.Shaffron	
D.A.Singer	
J.P.Veaner	
Mrs.Ben Kahn,	02-01-1914
M.Alper,	03-01-1914
Sol Bromberg	09-01-1914
Mrs.E.E.Ephraim	
Mrs.P.Stein	
S.J.Shaffron,	09-18-1914
Sol Fridner	
N.Schwartz,	04-08-1919

B.Wiesenthal
J.H.Robinson
Sol Blum,   09-15-1919
Jos Knapp
Adrian Levy
J.L.Souza

There now occurs a gap in the record of new members found in the minutes.

Paul Jacobson,   12-31-1938
Max Baum
Albert I.Clark, MD
Sam Farb
Ansel Kahn
Murray Klater
Henry Hecht
Aubrey Hirsch
Ruth Lake
Abe E.Levy
Morris Plantowsky
H.H.Morris
J.F.Seinsheimer, Jr.
Dr.A.Levy
Mrs.J.Lipson
Ben Wade
Charles Myron,   07-08-1940
Sanford Friedman
Sam Lebowitz
Joe Rosenfield
Harry Stevenson
Bernard Mayer
Harry Melcer
Ben Lipnick,   10-13-1941
Herbert Garon
Mike Mesinger

R.S.Polsky
Morris Schneider
J.T.Caesar
Miss.Ray Brown
Miss.Mary Brown
Henry Himlet
J.J.Utiz, Jr.
Sig Block
Moise Levy,   05-11-1942
Alfred Suhler,   09-08-1942
Frank Herman
Dr.Wm.Levine (Levin)
Stanford Weiner
A.R.Warren
Irving Saltz
Beulah Fischer
D.R.Carb
Ida Kotin
Isadore Graber
Mrs.Gail Seidl
Pearl Kotin
Mrs.Pauline Loeb
Abe Seibel,   12-14-1942
Charles Lerman
Ludwik Anigstein,   4-12-1943
Maurice Schapiro
Ralph Block,   10-11-1943
Adolph Katz,   12-13-1943
Max Leaman,   10-09-1944
Norman Nasits
Leon Jacobson
Paul Jacobson
Fred Davis
Paul Lee
Adrian Levy, Jr.   06-10-1946
Fannye Goldsmith,   09-09-1946
Harry A.Levine

Sidney Fisher
Alan Lipson
Marvin Stein
Simon Goldhirsch
Ben Patch
Ray Cohn
Maurice Schwartz
Alfred Tocker,   10-14-1946
Joe Nussenblatt
Sol Waag
Hyman Epstein
Herbert Mesinger
John Levy
Simon Miron,   12-17-1946
Robert Zander
Jack Nasts
Bernard Richmond,   04-14-1947
M.Plonsky
Alex Kottwitz
Sam Cohen
Jean Slopnicke,   06-09-1947
Ben Kotin
Peter Kamin
Leon Knapp
Ellis Levine
Louis Peters,   09-08-1947
Saul Hammer
Leon Segal
J.A.Davis,   10-14-1947
Raymond Garfield
Mrs.H.Heidenheimer
E.Wechsler
Mrs.Annie Minck
Julian Blum,   12-08-1947
Stanford Wernar
S.R.Shaffer,   10-11-1948
Seymour Shwiff

Emma Seinsheimer,	10-11-1948
Edythe Seinsheimer	
Louis Leavencrown,	11-08-1948
Arthur Neff	
Leon Roth,	12-13-1948
Ted Schreiber	
Gladys Kempner,	01-10-1949
Donald Susan,	04-12-1949
A.Ringel,	09-12-1949
Sam Spiegel	
H.Gerson	
Fred Heman	
Louis Baskind	
S.Silverman,	10-10-1949
L.Plantowsky	
I.Spasser	
Louis Druss	
Joe Ginsburg	
M.l.Ruben	
Ruben Clark,	01-09-1950
Abe Posnansky,	03-13-1950
Dale Carpenter,	10-14-1950
A.L.Selig	
Fannie Levy,	02-12-1951
Mrs.E.Heathersly,	09-10-1951
H.D.Massin	
Nathan Doner	
A.R.Schwartz	
Ben Brown,	10-08-1951
Hyman Ginsburg	
I.Shulman,	10-10-1951
Harry Melcer,	01-14-1952
A.L.Heine	
Licoln Strauss,	04-21-1952
Mrs.Ira Krow,	09-08-1952
I.Ippmann	
Seymour Richbook	

Emanuel Rosenblatt
Al Dricks,   11-10-1952
I.J.Graber
Ramon Borenstein
Aaron Yambra,   12-08-1952
M.Selik
Charles Molho
Henry Hecht
Harry Melcer,   03-09-1953
Robert Zander,   04-13-1953
James Branaum
Ben Doner,   10-12-1953
Henry Jameson
Henry Stern,   10-12-1953
Raymond Rosenberg
Esther Carval
Fred Hurwitz
Harry Sinagirb,   09-09-1957
Leon Bromberg
Alan Rosen
Harry Levy, III
Robert Mendelsohn,   10-09-1957
Richard Thurm,   11-11-1957
Mrs.Philip Jacobson
Leonard Pittel
Charles Molho,   02-10-1958
Sol Forman,   08-06-1958
Louis Levin,   09-08-1958
Sam Waldman
Warren Bender
Marvin Waskow
Stanley Levy
Lothar Salomon
Harry Weiser
Nathan Braslau
Eva Dorfman
Leon Bialostozky,   10-13-1958

Fannie Wilson,   01-12-1959
Ethel Sheffel
Samule Kolmen,   05-09-1959
William Irving
Joe Harr
Robert Hauser,   08-19-1959
Nathan Laufman
Lew Leitner
Ivan Goldman
Armond Goldman
Meyer Bronstein,   09-14-1959
Arthur Freeman
Floyd Melman
Neal Nathan
Marcus Neiger
Edward Wechsler
Anita Zinn
Norman Lerner
Joe Lerner
Arnold Nitishin
Norman Wilson
Sam Baum
Aaron Littmann
Harry Shay,   09-12-1960
Milton Altschuler
D.M.Winick,   10-10-1960
Arnold Weissler,   11-14-1960
Phillip Kocen
Martin Schneider
Henri Stahl,   02-13-1961
Gerlad WEiser,   10-09-1961
Steven Goldberg,   04-09-1962
Ralph Block,   04-01-1963
Mrs.Selma Snider,   09-09-1963
Harris Block
A.E.Rodin
Jack Alperin

Melvyn Gross
David Gold
Robert Gilgar
Arnold Drake
Harry Levy, II
Itaska Weinstein,   05-18-1964
Herbert Davis
Morris Clark,   09-04-1964
Mrs.Joseph Palmer
Mrs.Ben Brown
George Straty,   10-12-1964
Ben Kotin
Abe Levy
Murry Epstein,   01-11-1965
David Detmar,   04-12-1965
Samuel Freedman
Nathan Sukiennik,   11-11-1965
Alfred Dricks
Leonard Levine,   09-12-1966
Malcolm Mazow
Sylvan Boin,   09-11-1967
Ray Galloup,   10-09-1967
Kermit Meade
Hannan Schwiff
R.L.Marcus
Harry Freedman
Bernard Lyons,   11-13-1967
Mrs.Joseph Godfrey
William Helfman
Charles Molho
Ben May,   10-14-1968
Robert Trieff,   10-13-1969
Aaron Cohen
Robert Brotman,   11-10-1969
Herman Sigel
Fred Abrams,   02-09-1970
Eugene Hornstein

Theresa Heatherly,	05-11-1970
Barry Portnoy,	08-10-1970
Gary Schechter,	08-10-1970
Byron Wilkenfield	
Hope Kotin	
James Herman,	09-14-1970
David Dochen	
Morton Leonard,	11-09-1970
Robert Roth	
Bernard Bloom	
Steve Greenberg,	04-12-1971
Harold Levine,	09-13-1971
David Joel	
D.H.Martin	
Al Levinson,	12-13-1971
Harry Croft	
E.R.Thompson, Jr.	
Mike Warren	
Albert Pittel,	05-08-1972
Arthur Lipton,	06-12-1972
Lawrence Jacobson,	09-11-1972
Gerald Suhler	
Rose Spector	
Hanan Swiff	
Andrew Kant	
Morris Pollock	
Allan Goldstein	
Sam Bormaster	
Linda McDonald,	10-09-1972
Richard Markham,	12-11-1972
Seymour Richbook	
Charles Gray,	03-12-1973
Sidney Schochet,	10-08-1973
Henry Bergman	
Robert Zuzak	
Jordan Staffin	
Lillie Gorman,	11-13-1973

Sonya Stanton
Jerome Goldstein,   02-11-1974
Jill Pinsker
Martin Risk,   04-08-1974
Simon Rapp,   06-10-1974
Morton Leonard,   07-08-1974
Abe Hauser,   08-12-1974
Roger Schwartz,   09-09-1974
Sam Platt
Joseph Metz
Michael Berger,   10-14-1974
Nick Harris
Meyer Reiswerg
Arnold Skor
Irwin Novak
Robert Davis,   10-14-1974
Joe Brecher,   11-11-1974
Harvey Levin
Jack Moreas
Nancy Shear
Maury Kleinman,   12-09-1974
Gerson Bloom,   01-13-1975
Mrs.Ben Suhler,   02-10-1975
Nathan Sukiennik,   03-10-1975
Julian Levy
Brent Masel,   08-11-1975
Jeffrey Rossio
Stuart De Camp
Jerome Elman
Steven Schwartz
Sharon Wellons,   09-08-1975
Vic Bastron,   10-03-1975
Marvin Cannon
Nancy Kneisley
Allan Mandell
Leah Rae Miron
Max Nevelow

Donald Roache
Alvin Schneider
Larry Waters
Arthur Chausmer
Felix Meyer,   11-10-1975
Sandy Schreiber
Robert J.Golden
Stephen Newmark
Richard Marks,   12-08-1975
Tanya Forman,   01-12-1976
Joe Schlankey,   03-08-1976
David Schwarz   10-13-1976
Morrie Pearlman
Patti Edelman   09-13-1976
Martin Rappaport   01-10-1977
Ted Schwartz
Barbara Ozon   02-14-1977
Estelle Osborne
Lorraine Sharon   04-11-1977
Gerald Golden   08-13-1977
Peter Lazarus
Richard Slavin   09-19-1977
Rosalie Schwarz   10-10-1977
Joel Berman   12-12-1977
Mary McCutchen
Robert Rose   01-09-1978
Raymond Rosenberg   07-10-1978
Ed Erde   08-14-1978
Jai Burnes   09-11-1978
Marilyn Brodwick
Daniel Gold   10-9-1978
Barbara Crews
Irving Slavin   12-11-1978
Judith Abplanap
Darwin Winick
Jordan Finkelstein   02-12-1979
Betty Nevelow   06-11-1979

133

Sandy Rubin	09-20-1979
Julian Kitay	11-12-1979
Steve Allen	
Gayle Kamen	
David Smith	02-11-1980
Harry Wallfish	
Douglas Harrison	05-12-1980
Michael Gruber	07-14-1980
Fred Hurwitz	08-11-1980
Victor Miller	09-08-1980
Bruce Leipzig	
Gerald Suhler	
Murray Epstein	
Clara Hillman	10-13-1980
Martin Risk	
Harold Herman	
Myron Heimlich	
Martha Bernfeld	11-10-1980
Michael Manheimer	12-08-1980
Malcom Brodwick	03-11-1981
Frances Nussbaum	
Dale Wadatz	04-13-1981
Bruce Hicken	05-10-1981
Dorothy Swann	
Sam Clark	1981
Sheryl Leonard	
Ira Ipman	1981
Emanuel Littmann	
Mrs. Abe Pozmantier	
Ben Schneider	
Mrs. Morris Schneider	
Mark Schrier	
Kevin Katz	06-14-1982
Sharon Levy Pagan	10-11-1982
Steven Malkin	
Joshua Wilkenfeld	
James Selig	11-08-1982

Dov Freedman
Bernard Demoratsky
Susan Lipnick Walsh
Philip Lipnick
Philip Jameson
Barbara Sasser   12-13-1982
Errol Kalmaz
Harris Labowitz
Anita Klein
Vernon Friedland   01-10-1983
Robert Lynch   05-09-1983
Karen Beasley
Andrew Barenberg
Mr. Yusim   06-13-1983
Aaron Katz
Ronnie Ginsberg   09-12-1983
David Jameson
Mr. Nash
Wanda Golding   10-10-1983
Alvin Soloman
Richard Dreyfus
Jeffrey Lisse   12-12-1983
Sonya Findlay   02-13-1984
Rudy Roden
Elise Frankfort   04-09-1984
David Schiff
Harold Herman   10-08-1984
Joel Blumberg   1985
Peter Atkins
David Bessman
Rakhil Yusim
Wayne Tolliver
Haskell Farb
Thomas Cole
Shirley Freed
Joel Schulman
Sanford Fineman

Anthony Scott	
Isidoro Beraja	
Lynn Cantini	05-12-1986
Darryl Levy	08-11-1986
William Meshel	
Ben Saltz	
Andrew Mytelka	
Janet Hassinger	
David Simmons	
Newt Scott	
John Gordon	
Babette Gugenheim	11-10-1986
Lewis Rosen	
Henry Cittone	
David Davis	
Abe Levy	
Gordon Klein	03-09-1987
Scott Supowit	
Sherman Kottle	05-11-1987
Mrs. Nathan Braslau	
Lawrence Goodman	
Ely Finkel	07-13-1987
Merrill Reuter	12-14-1987
Robert Goldhirsh	
Larry Sokolic	
Charlene Jouett	
Marilyn Chambers	03-14-1988
Etta Kuefner	
Lawrence Menache	05-09-1988
Irving Ducoff	
Simon Goldhirsh	08-08-1988
Leslie Hill	10-10-1988
Marilyn Schultz	
Ben Gelman	
Allan Hurwitz	07-17-1989
Irvin Slavin	08-14-1989
Nat Shapiro	07-13-1992

Blanche Alter	09-10-1992
Sam Nussenblatt	
Mike Pryor	
Marc Katz	
Ira Brotman	10-12-1992
Marla Kenney	
Cindy Bowes	
Robert Hirschfeld	
Robert Safirstein	11-06-1992
Brent Richbook	12-14-1992
Marc Kudisch	04-12-1993
Ronald Shapiro	
Craig Eichler	06-14-1993
Sherry Hafferty	09-13-1993
Michael Brandon	
Neil Levin	
Stanley Faber	
Pica Kahn	
Stephen Marx	
Steve Resnick	10-11-1993
Daniel Shane	
David Swiff	
Janet Hassinger	
Danny Carson	
Ivan Zador	12-13-1993
Andrea Parker	
David Schwarz	
Paul Smith	
Roger Soloway	
Virginia Fernandez	01-10-1994
Benjamin Gojer	02-14-1994
Wayne O'Quin	04-11-1994
Jeffrey Kramer	06-13-1994
David Cutler	08-08-1994
Albert Kheradpour	02-12-1996
Allan Fradkin	03-11-1996
Debra Thomson	04-08-1996

Sacha Jacobson	05-13-1996
Julie Jacobson	
Leslie Warren	09-09-1996
Karen Brandreth	
Fannie Romick	
Sari Kotin	
Alan Slay	10-14-1996
Marilyn Schultz	
Jack Isaacson	
Amanda Walters	
David Trieff	07-14-1997
William Scholl	01-12-1998
Debra Valastro	
Phyllis Jendrusch	02-09-1998
Sidney Croft	09-14-1998
Joseph Vinetz	
Marla Kenney	
Mindy Hilser	10-12-1998
Mitch Wilson	11-09-1998
Karylin Harr	12-14-1998
Patricia Romick	01-11-1999
Donna Weaver	04-12-1999
Rita Pack	05-10-1999
William Posnick	09-13-1999
Martin Archer	10-11-1999
Giere Boyd	
Kenny Herz	
Myles Reich	11-08-1999
Alice Schabe	
Steve Windsor	12-13-1999
Ben Dwoskin	
David Evans	02-14-2000
Lawrence Baum	06-12-2000
Ruth Soulsby Monroy	11-13-2000
Martin Colman	12-11-2000
Deborah Walenta	01-08-2001
Amy Sachs	02-12-2001

Joseph Barnett	05-14-2001
Alice O'Quin	
Bert Reiner	07-09-2001
Todd Masel	09-10-2001
Ted Ginsberg	
Terra Holdeman	
Sarah Keith	
Lisa Rubin	
Charles Peters	10-15-2001
Jennifer Bard	
Jay Green	11-12-2001
Birdie Cohn	02-11-2002
Bernard Dombrow	06-10-2002
Kevin Burke	09-09-2002
Deborah Taylor	10-14-2002
Jody Stein	
Michael Shinder	
Deborah Elkon	11-11-2002
Cheryl Kaplan	
Jennifer Mineo	03-10-2003
Steve Katz	04-14-2003
Vlad Listengarden	08-11-2003
Melanie Herz	10-13-2003
Milton Abelow	
Steven Feldman	

Confirmands of Temple B'nai Israel

The following is the most complete list of confirmands of Temple B'nai Israel for the inclusive dates.

May 21, 1874

Marvin Levy, Joseph Wenar, Sigmund Epstein, Nathan Blumenkron, Albert Wurzberger, Estella Cohn, Era Meyer, Lizzie Labatt, Lena Wurzberger, Flora Levy.

February 21, 1875

Adolph Cohn, Mollie Levy, Rosa Wenar, Estelle Schramm, Rachel Blumenkorn, Nellie Barnett, Mathilda Schessinger, Rosa Levy, Clara Lewis, Nattie Posner.

May 17, 1877

Maurine Block, Julia Michael, Halda Oberstein, Fanny Gross, Meyer, Gustave Dreyfus.

May 27, 1879

Henrietta Goldstein, Charlotte Dreyfus, Caroline Meyer, Julius Wurzburger, Lion Josner, Henry Meyer.

May 10, 1880

Alice Samuels, Leila Frank, Carline Rosenfield, Henry Posnainsky, Louis Levy, Charles Davis.

April 15, 1881

Sam Block, Harry Dreyfus, Raoul Dreyfus, Clara Wollstein, Cecile Sapson, Rosa Halff, Bettie Levy, Justine Haas.

June 5, 1889

Isaac Lovenberg, Isaac Rosenfield, Morris Frenkel, Bella Sonnenthiel, Selma Predecka, Rose Wenk, Bertha Levy, Annie Lord, Jennie Samuels, Julia Blum.

May 25, 1890

Miriam Rosenfield, Jennie Mansberg, Julia Blum, Carrie Marx, Bertha Cohen, Rosa Predecka, Melanie Kauffman, Ethel Weingerger, Jennie Cohen.

June 12, 1891

Elka Freeman, Helen Sonnenthiel, Sara Feist, Annie Wenk, Harby Frank, Benjamin Schram, Moses Harris, Ben Frenkel.

June 1, 1892

Leonora Lion, Blanche Rosenfield, Lonora Samuels, Fleurette Lovenberg, Theresa Harris, Henry Blumbargh.

May 21, 1893

Cordella Lewis, Rachel Kory, Rica Hertzfeld, Albert Lasker, Bertha Block, Evelyn Levy.

June 10, 1894

Frederick Werb, Morris Block, Phillip Osterman, Samuel Lovenberg, Laurence SAmuels, Ralph J.Schwarz,

Carrie Blum, Coralie Block, Minna Levy, Rosa Levy, Julia Klugman, Irene Levy, Henrietta Waag, Louisa Blum, Annie Flatto, Irene Ullmann, Theresa Stern.

May 18, 1896

Rosa Block, Sadie Hershfield, Bertha Meyer, Lillian Samuel, Edna Lewis, Carrie Levy, Abraham Freed, Mithcel Marsberg, Joseph Cohen, Leon Meyer, Charles Ostermann, Julius Weinberger.

June 6, 1897

Solomon Levy, Clarence Rosenfield, Leon Caston, Solomon Waag, Samuel Cohen, Cecilia Block, Julia Marx, Carrie Stein, Hattie Cohen, Ernestine Levy, Core Weis.

May 27, 1898

Sadie Baer, Rosetta Miller, Henrietta Blum, Florince Lasker, Esther Katz, Beatrice Levy, Max Maas, Alphonse Block, Jake Levy.

September 12, 1902

Clara Celia Zinn, R.I.Cohen, Jr., Esther Osterman, Millie Freed, Bertha Lillian Miller, Rebecca Sarah Sacovich.

June 1, 1903

Lillian Blum, Clarence Schornstein, Fannie Miller, Leon Bonart, Hyman L.Block, Hyman G.Meyer, Julia B.Blum, Minnie B.Kauffman, Minnie Goodman, Leah J.Schornstein, Gertrude Schornstein, Lillian E.Herz, Bertha I.Himler, Esther Thompson, Loula D.Lasker, Fannie Kempner, Julia Evelyn Levy, Beulah J.Miller Anna H.Maas.

May 19, 1904

Sara Blum, Yetta Rauch, Berty Slavsky, Fannie Samuels, Matilda Littman, Ervie Levy, Elsie Brock, Morris Meyer, Samuel Weinberger, Frances Osterman, Hermena Deiches.

June 9, 1905

Margaret Littman, Julia Levy, Sadie Meyer, Ruth Cohen, Lillian Driches, Irwin Herz, Bertha Ephraim, Rosa Gordon, Mary Silvers, Henrietta Moscowitz, Sara Kempner, Chas.Bonart.

May 30, 1906

Fred Mayer, Sol Rosenberg, Marion Levy, Isadore Freed, Aline Raphael, Barbara Gernsbacher, Gertrude Block, Sadie Block.

May, 1907

John Levy, R.Levy, Elinor Jacob, Helen Rosenfield, Clarence Lewis, Louis Gernsbacher, Florance Bonart, Isaac Lippmann.

June 5, 1908

Lizzie Dorfman, Rosa Knapp, Ethel Ullman, Belle Pearl, Annie Geller, Leopold Schornstein, Leopold Meyer, Lottie Breslau, Samuel Robinson, Hyman Dreyfus, Edna Schwartz, Rose Mehrbach.

1909

Esther Hauser, Gladys Cohen, Geo.Moscowitz, Clarence Milhauser, Harry Cohen, Theresa Wansker, Esther Bonart, Ruth Schornstein, Selma Wansker, Leopold Walters.

1910

Dorothy Littman, Meyer Blankfield, Gertrude Mayer, Maggie Oshman, Richard Schornstein, Julia Levy, Lillian Ephraim, Sadie Dreeben, Blance Block.

1911

Elinor Morris, Rachael Schreiber, Marguarite Meyer, Julius Blankenfield, Maurice Moskowitz, Hedie Bonart, Fred Zander, John Frenkel, Camille Bernheim, Mary Massin, Esther Buchwald, Harry Jacobs, Joe Heyman.

1914

Helen Sampson.Helen Adams, Estelle Bromberg, Alphonse Bernheim, Sadie Buchwald, Leon Bromberg, Arthur Meyer, Ethel Krulewich, Fannie Rosenberg, Ida Diamond.

1915

Robert Zander, Yetta Schreiber, Teanie Sakowitz, Sylvia Brown, Herman Heyman, Esther Littmann, Leon Gutman, Margaret Guttman, Marvin Kahn, Esther Block, Hyman Stollmack, Clothilde Morris.

June 6, 1916

Eleanor Abbot, Anna Buchwald, Migel Krulewich, Dorothy King, Rose Blankfield, Betty Stahl, Yetta Rosenberg, Lottie Blark, Sidney Baskin.

1917

Morris Schreiber, Ida Rosenthal, Belle Buchwald, Esther Meyer, Aimee Bernheim, Alec Sakowitz, Carrie Block, Marjorie Klein, Ruth Waag, Hazel Rauch, Ben Waag, Alphonse Meyer.

1918

Nathan Diamond, Leonore Raphael, Freida Schreiber, Ida Rosenberg, Herbert Frapart, Esther Massin, Abraham Rosenberg, Rebecca O'Donnell, Agnes Zander, Gilbert Krulewich, Malvin Wolff.

1919

Nathan Braslau, Janice Nevelow, Leon Blum, Eva Rosenthal, Ann Rosenthal, Clara Kerson, Gertrude Block, Meyer Sakowitz, Ella Kerpel, Esther Guttman.

1920

Bertha Rosetnthal, Bertha Clark, Harry Klein, Bessie Herold, Hiawera O'Donnell, Rosabelle Blum, Grace Sampson Isadore Speigel.

1921

Natalie Schwartz, Emma Greenberg, Dorothy Sakowitz, Marion Levy, Sam Speigel, Libbye Fradkin, Adam Levy, Lillian Abbott, Edward Schreiber.

1922

Bernard Kauffman, Israel Schreiber, Abe Guttman, Fannie Hochman, Harry Alberga, Thyra Alberga, Louise Buchwald, Joe Block.

1923

Ida Kaminsky, Mathilda Posmantier, Bettie Nevelow, leah Hochman, Mae Leitner, Doris Harris, Jennie Sakowitz, Frances Newman, Morris Schneider, Ralph Block, Jennie Teicher, Ben Clark, Florence Levy, Aaron Littmann, Ben Krandel, Gertrude Katz.

1924

Louis Leitner, Ben Levy, S.a.Levy, Martha Teicher, Ruth Keison, Norman Clark, Rose Oshman, Hannah Kaminsky, Henry Melcer, Beatrice Newman, Mike Mitchell.

1925

Louis Thompson, Geraldine Levy, Rose Baum, Bertha

Levy, Bernice Rosenthal, Tillie Haus, Helene Samuels, Sarah Landesman, DAvid Shapiro, Bertha Passman, Hirsh Schwartz, Mildred Littmann, Irving Abeloro.

1926

Emanuel Littmann, Majorie Kauffman, Julian Levy, Theresa Kauffman, Louis Druss, Dearia Minck, Nina Braslau, Bertha Kaminsky, Frank Nussbaum, Gertrude Pozmantier, Max Levy, Julian Blum.

1927

Ida Nevelow, Robert I.Cohen, III, Pearl Lerner, Leon Weiss, Gertrude Saltz, Marie Aronsfeld, Sam Passman, Irving Weinstein, Mildred Teicher, Max Phillips, Herman Shapiro, Barbara Kaufman.

1928

Ida Saltz, Tillie Leitner, Etta Kauffman, Bessie Nathan, Rose Knapp, Elsie Hochman, Leonora Kempner, Nettie Rundell, Donald Winter, Sara Swiff.

1929

Majorie Brock, Rose Bronstein, Rebecca Druss, Clara Feldman, Rose Flegenheimer, Sol Harr, Emanuel Hochman, Leon Jacobson, Reba Kerson, Eli Leman, Sadye Leaman, Audrey Levy, Etta Nathan, Blanche Schneider, Harry Schreiber, J.Fellman Seinsheimer, Sadie Trifon, Sadie Weiner.

1930

Harold Brecher, Myrtle Faden, Sidney Fisher, Rose Framer, Peter Kaminsky, Henrietta Kauffman, Harry Kirscher, Peter Oshman, Esther Saltz, Anna Swiff.

1931

Henrietta Block, Clara Baum, Pearl Handler, Sara Kerson, Bertha Levy, Lassie Posnick, Fannie Melcer, Pauline Phillips, Edna Winter, J.M.Heidenheimer, Max Leaman, Abe Levy, Sam Nussenblatt, Jake Smith, Alfred Tocker, Bernard Tinterow.

1932

Lottie Agranowitz, Esther Bergman, Florence Borofsky, Lillian Braslau, Lee Ducoff, Ben Druss, Dorothy Holste, Frances Kay, Dorothy Kerson, Frieda Lang, Ruth Levy, Jean Nussbaum, Minnie Plantowsky, Bella Rotenberg, Irwin Waltz, Meyer Tinterwo, Sophie Zalichin.

1933

Iving Ducoff, Stanley Fisher, Sidney Handler, Daniel Kauffman, Dorothy Kerson, Esther Landesman, Marion J.Levy, Jr., Evelyn Lipnick, John niethe, Eugene Nevelow, Maurice Rosofsky, Henry Suhler, Majorie Todes, Edwin Weiss.

1934

Anna Levy, Sadye Saltz, Dorothy Fradkin, Fannie Machles, Miriam Roth, Sarah Plantowsky, Bernice Braslau, Edmond Frapart, Harry Rosenthal, Winston Hidenheimer, Alfred Suhler, George Kirschner, Stanley Firestein.

1935

Ruth Lake, Lassie Greenberg, Felice Weill, Lillian Knapp, Helen Holste, Muriel Faden, Idalee Mandel, Meyer Levy, Sam J.Rosenfield, Simon Goldhirsh, Adele Fridner, Adrian Levy, Jr., Adele Landesman.

1936

Eugene Heidenheimer, Joseph Oshman, Harry Swiff, Joseph Ducoff, Laura Plonsky, Bertha Jacobs, Zelda Zinn, Ruth Machles, Helen Harr, Dorothy Braslau, Clara Plantowsky, Estelle Rogers, Rosa Leaman, Dorothy Levy, Hortense Davidson, Ethel Kerson, Edna Seinsheimer.

1937

Ida Kotin, Pearl Kotin, Richard Cohen, Ruth Holste, Roslyn Block, Doris Novin, Rosalie Kerson, Eva Landesman, Sara Plantowsky, Jeanette Pozmantier.

1938

Joy Cohen, Symour Swiff, Sylvia Ducoff, Estelle Levy, Golda Plantowsky, Patsy Hellman, Gertrude Weiner, Minnie Kerson.

1939

Natalie Zinn, Annalee Knapp, Lillian Jacobs, Esther Moskowitz, Frances Goldhirsh, Betty Davidson, Joyce Schreiber, Gloria Levy, Harris Block, Louis Isenberg, Jerry Melamed.

1940

Samona Bodansky, Clara Brecher, Natalie Moskowitz, Lois Rosenfield, Irving Clark, Howard Knapp, Jean Nierman, Max Jevy, Jr., Maurice Nevelow, Carol Perlman.

1941

Natalie Joel, Sam S.Kay, Jr., Renee Coppersmith, Roger Martinelli, Sylvia Nevelson, Milton Sampson, Bayla Lippman, Bernice Knapp.

1942

Edis Martinelli, Henry Cohen, Alfred Rosenfield, Clara Suhler.

1943

Sam Clark, Idalee Kahn, Fred Holste.

1944

Charlotte Moskowitz, Sylvia Levy, Ruth Martinelli, Louis Plantowsky, Joan Nusbaum, Estelle Holste.

1945

Ruth Bodansky, Norman Braslau, Charles Gerson, Elbert Joel, Tarris Joel, Arline Kay, Gordon Kirschner, Carolyn Nathan, Seymour Nussenblatt, Marvin Swiff, Mamie Suhler, Bobbie Tocker, Anita Zinn, Robert Zinn.

1947

Harriett Levy, Hallene Fargotstein, Marilyn Nierman, George Sampson, Robert Anigstein, Richard Wells.

1948

Shirley Plantowsky, Rosemary Isenberg, Neil Nathan, Robert Braslau, Paul White, Edward Jacobs, Harold Levy.

1949

M.Robert Hecht, Sandy Schreiber, Harris Labowitz, Edward Hecht, Annette Fargotstein, David Braslau, Jerry Wells, Merle Zinn, Elton Lipnick, Ruth McCoy.

1950 (Adult Class)

Alice Block, Sadell Clark, Peter Oshman, Sam Rosenstein, Stan Beitman.

1951

Harry Levy, III, Maureen Schreiber.

1952

Phyllis Braslau, Stanley Levy, Rosanne Perlman, Irwin Kay, Stanley Kottwitz.

1953

Sonya Lipnick, Allan Graber, Barbara Clark, Walter Hecht, Reda Porin, Aaron Sampson.

1955

Elka Fargotstein, Ronald Graber, Irwin M.Herz, Jr., Doris Katz, Marlene Nathan.

1956

Paul Burka, Susan Graber, Jeneene Krantz, Jason Perlman, Ella Roth, Michael Nussenblatt.

1958

Lynda Doner, John Harris, Norma Herman, Jerry Kottwitz, Gerry Levin, Harvey Pollard, Rochelle Saltz, David Suhler.

1960

Karen Gerson, Tracy Harris, Nancy Kauffman, Sheila Krantz, Jerome Lipnick, Monty Patch, Max Roth, David Swiff.

1961

Cheryl Baum, Harriette Clark, Richard Graber, Gary Lerner, Marilyn Levy, Jonathan Littmann, Felix Meyer, Carol Pollard, Joan Schenk, Nancy Schneider, Gerald Suhler.

1962

Sharon Brown, Jane Burka, Benay Clark, Jerald Jacobson, Elaine Kay, Carol Levin, Richard May, Wesler Perlman, Herbert Yambra.

1963

Dianna Gilman, David Ginsburg, Sharon Graber, Elizabeth Jameson, Barbara Krantz, Susan Lipnick, Leo Niger, Susan Plantowsky, Marilyn Saltz, Stephen Schneider.

1964

Beverly Demoratsky, Greta Herman, Cynthia Kay, Philip Lipnick, Leah Rae Miron, Judith Plantowsky, James Richbook, Mark Stein, Sandra Sussan.

1965

Steven Ginsburg, Edwin Graber, Alice Jameson, Murray Lerner, Alan Nussenblatt, Gail Patch, Benita Rosenblatt.

1966

Barbara Block, Bennie Dorfman, Donalyn Epstein, Rikki Goldhirsh, Robert Goldshirsh, Andrea Kay, Neil perlman, Marlene Plantowsky, Barbara Rosenberg, Lezli Ruben, Madeline Selig, Ben Jay Stein, Ronnie Yambra.

1968

Norienne Ginsberg, Roberta Klein, Michael Miron, Marsha Rosenberg, Stefani Ruben, Debby Selig, David Jameson, Michael Leitner, Bonnie Plantowsky, Judith Rosenbloom, Ben Saltz, Janet Sussan.

1979

Jody Baron, Jennifer Goldstein, Leah Golden, Teddy Schreiber, and Tim Thompson

May 15, 1994

Heather Leonard, Jacqueline White, Michelle White, Adam Druss, Robbie Fradkin, Jacob Gelman, Ben Wallfisch, Russin Royal, Benjy Shabot, Beth Goldblum, and Libbie Bessman

May 19, 1996

Asher Royal, Amy Leonard, Sarah Shabot, Sara Wall-fisch, Erin Reiswerg, Brian Masel, and Nathan Pryor

May, 1998

Daniel Goodman, David Supowit, Clay Gongora, Lauren Freedman, Emily Gellman, Seth Katz, Heather Hill, Samantha Clark, Matthew Bessman, and Jenny Rochkind

May, 2000

Andy Kessler, Emily Sasser, Kevin Goodman, James Kenney, and Chase Katz

May, 2002

Jenny Kessler, Aaron Brandon, Elly Harrison, Rochelle March, Richard Dricks, Jana Ginsberg, Whitney Fields, Michael Sasser, and Heather Hess

Marriages at Temple B'nai Israel

These are the records of marriages at the Temple. Unfortunately they were only recorded up through 1911 and aren't complete.

Date	Parties
4-18-1869	B.Goodman,Levy of Navasota
6-7-1869	Isaac Reinauer, Rebecca Weise
1-20-1870	I.Bedach,Miss Bertha James
9-21-1870	Levy Ehrenfeld, Sophie Levy
10-9-1870	B.H.Jacobs, Ida Kory
3-15-1871	Randolph Carrow, Caroline Meyer
6-7-1871	Alphonse Levy, Lizzie Gartner
7-5-1871	M.Mayman, Adele Kauffman
11-16-1871	Solomon Halft, Fannie Lewis
11-19-1871	Simon Mayer, Augusta Weis
12-13-1871	P.H.Morris, Meina Vogel
1- -1872	J.Rosenberg, Leah Rosenberg
1-8-1873	Gustave Feist, Rosa Harris
4-6-1873	Louis Loellner, Emma Stiffell
4-9-1873	Jacob Sonnentheil, Sallie Levy
4-9-1873	Emmanuel Tillmann, Franzisca Stess
11-5-1873	Max Maas, Sarah Davis

8-16-1874	Marx Marcus, Augusta Lulka
9-13-1874	Philip Freeman, Theodocia Rushing
10-6-1874	H.Seligman, Eliza Suss
2-10-1875	Isadore Lovenberg, Jennie Samuels
12-15-1875	M.E.Friedlander, Clara Levy
3-30-1876	Solomon Levine, Sarah Epstein
4-26-1876	M.Lasker, Nettie Davis
9-13-1876	J.S.Rosenfield, Theresa Hilb
11-8-1876	David Freeman, Mary Geinsberg
1-14-1877	Godchaux Levi, Theresa Gugenheim
2-7-1877	Joseph Nussbaum, Claire Neroman
4-11-1877	Ben Levy, Flora Schram
4-25-1877	Frederick Beckhardt, Henrietta Longrin
5-2-1877	D.Steiner, Henrietta Levy
5-9-1877	David Dreeben, Ella May Ruth
5-16-1877	R.Loeb, Rosa Lochstenstein
8-15-1877	Leopold Block, Fanny Cahn
10-3-1877	L.Loew, Blanche Wolff
10-24-1877	Samuel Roos, Adele Katz
3-9-1878	Aaron Waag, Charlotte Auerbach
5-21-1878	M.Kauffman, Henriett Jacobs
5-21-1878	Theodor H.Hinder, Fanny Meyer
10-16-1878	Emanuel Samuels, Rosa Kahn
12-4-1878	Adolph Harris, Fanny Grumbach
2-27-1879	I.Franklin, Rebecca Cohn
3-19-1879	Jos.Seinsheimer, Blanche Fellman
5-26-1879	Nathan Relich, R.O.Maas
5-26-1879	Siegfried Schwarz, Sarah Doucey
6-8-1879	M.A.Hirsch, Mathilde Aschheim
6-18-1879	Baruch Levy, Helen Auerbacher
3-10-1880	Achille Meyer, Malline Kahn
3-24-1880	Moses Freiberg, Nora Eldridge

1880	Charles B.Miller, Estelle Schram
1880	Mark Goldstein, Rosa Woolf
1880	Gus Levy, Molline Meyer
3-16-1881	Loewenstein Rockdale, Miss.Levine
5-25-1881	B.F.Caston, Sallie A.Sampson
10-12-1881	A.M.Rosenfield, Lena Wurzburger
2-15-1882	M.E.Lazorus, Flory P.Henrique
4-19-1882	Robert I.Cohen, Agnes Lord
4-26-1882	Emanuel Longini, Rosa Levy
9-6-1882	F.Milheiser, Clara Lord
10-11-1882	A.Rosenwald, Lina Haas
10-22-1882	J.Bernstein, Miss.Haas
1-2-1884	Paul Asher, Augusta Goldstein
1-9-1884	Isaac Cohen, Clara Lewis
3-12-1884	M.E.Tausack, Theresa Zander
3-26-1884	Bernhard Levy, Estella Block
4-2-1884	Robert Weis, Mamie Block
4-29-1884	Emanuel Untermeyer, Julia Michael
6-18-1884	Moritz T.Rogers, Rosa Lord
6-18-1884	Morris L.Riglander, Harriet Goldstein
7-16-1884	Jacob L.Miller, Anna Herz
10-26-1884	Jacob Schornstein, Jennie Arons
3-4-1885	Charles Loewenstein, Flora Kahn
1887	Henrietta Block,Rabbi Joseph Silverman
4-25-1888	Richard E.Seeligman, Zerlina Rosenfield
6-5-1888	S.Gernsbacher, Fannie Gross
3-4-1889	Meyer Schlinger, Katy Stern
5-1-1889	Rabbi A.Rosenberg, Rosa Meyer
5-8-1889	Hugo Lieberman, Leah Lieberman
9-7-1889	Lev Posner, Nettie Harris
11-1-1889	Herman Lazarus, Lena Schwarz
3-6-1889	Henry Cohen, Mollie Levy

3-5-1890	A.C.Raas, Katie Lord
3-20-1890	B.A.Isaacs, Bella Schram
7-13-1890	Mr.Gabert, Rilda Lewis
1-1-1891	Henry Cook, Fanny Lieberman
1-20-1891	M.C.Michael, Belle Weis
2-4-1891	S.J.Rosenfield, Carrie Levy
2-15-1891	M.Cohen, Nora Hirsch
5-7-1891	Moses Hirschfeld, Sophie Verblansky
6-9-1891	Isaac Harrison, Lena Gordon
9-20-1891	Sam Hellman, Fannie Posnainsky
10-27-1891	Louis W.Levy, Mattie Heidenheimer
1-4-1892	Julius Adam, Julia Heller
3-19-1892	J.Jacobs, Minnie Casselberg
10-13-1892	W.B.Seesking, Frances Weis
10-13-1892	Alex Kalensher, Tilla Fox
12-3-1892	Ignatz Goodman, Yetta Weil
12-26-1892	Karl Schwarz, Sophie Raphael
1-8-1893	J.Becker, Annie Burk
1-27-1893	Hermann Blankfield, Ethel Winkler
3-18-1893	Isaac Ehrlich, Harmina Lederier
6-21-1893	Mr.Nussbaum, Theresa Mayer
7-31-1893	Simon Marx, Julia Muller
8-11-1893	I.Frucht, Bertha Herr
12-29-1893	Alfred Levi, Bella Jacobs
1-10-1894	Ike Meyer, Julia Good
3-18-1894	Jonas Levy, Henrietta Klein
4-19-1894	Leon Mosbacker, Bertha Lord
10-17-1894	Wolfe Wenk, Miss.Weil
11-7-1894	Mr.Weil, Miss.M.Kauffman
9-11-1895	Edward Scharff, Esther Marx
10-20-1895	Jules Dreyfus, Maggie Tarter
11-5-1895	M.L.Malevinsky, Bella Maas

10-10-1895	Morris Joseph, Annie Farber
10-20-1895	Myron Goldman, Bertha Schwarz
12-17-1895	F.Guttmann, Flora Flatto
12-18-1895	Hermann Meyer, Estelle Levy
12-29-1895	Harry Saslavsky, Mary Blackman
1-31-1896	E.Pliner, Cecile Daitz
2-13-1896	Isaac Shinata, Fannie Bader
6-22-1896	Sam J.Hyman, Daisey Klugman
11-4-1896	Richard Weber, Kate Samuels
1-2-1897	Ernest M.Loeb, Elka Freeman
1-19-1897	Charles Rauch, Rebecca Angel
1-20-1897	Sam J.Levy, Mathilde Leon
4-27-1897	Sidney Reinhardt, Alice A.Blum
4-27-1897	S.L.Reinhardt, Fannie V.Blum
6-20-1897	Isadore Diamond, Fannie Hirsch
11-7-1897	Louis Himmelfarb, Anna Rosen
2-27-1898	Simon Louis, Ella Rudnick
3-5-1898	Mayer Krulewich, Fannie Migel
4-5-1898	J.Joseph, Minnie Stern
5-10-1898	Ben Burg, Bertha Wagner
8-8-1898	David S.Hart, Flora Wolf
9-28-1898	Jacob Morris, Hatti Morse
11-8-1898	Lev Jacobs, Camille Blum
12-14-1898	Jack Isaacs, T.Schram
1-1-1899	Louis Silberman, Tillie Laklien
9-17-1899	Emil Meyer, Esther Cohen Katz
11-14-1899	Emil Kahn, Yetta Glicksman
5-9-1900	Edward Pollack, Henrietta Waag
7-15-1900	Bernard Isaacs, Maynes Osterman
1-6-1901	Eph.Goldstein, Hattie Baer
4-19-1901	Sigmund Lass, Jennie Goldstein
5-7-1901	Harry H.Levy, Nettie L.Maas

6-30-1901	M.Tannnbaum, Miss Salavsky
3-16-1902	Ralph Frapart, Rosa Block
9-12-1902	Joe Epstein, Bessie Leiblum
12-17-1902	I.H.Kempner, Henrietta Blum
4-8-1903	Joseph Schwartz, Blance Heidenheimer
12-16-1903	H.Oppenheimer, Hattie Kempner
3-9-1904	Aaron Levy, Fannie Levy
3-5-1905	Sidney Meyer, Carrye Levy
6-6-1906	D.W.Kempner, Miss Bertig
3-1-1910	Herman Novinsky, Esther Nierman
10-16-1910	Mrs.Jonas Levy, Sam Fuchs
12-12-1910	Julius H.Green, Icie Osenbaugh
1911	Bernard Samuel, Julia Levy
1958	Rose Knapp, Alvah Davis
9-29-1963	Linda Zindler, Neil Nathan
1966	Benay Clark, Ben Blend
1966	Barabara Clark, Martin Schneider
1-4-1970	Cindy Kay, Robert Greenwood
12-31-72	Andrea Kay, Gary Parker
1976	Linda Allsen, Eric Nevelow
1977	Nancy Auger, Bruce Deifik
1977	Barbara Ozon, Donald White
1977	Shelley Nussenblatt, Rabbi Jimmy Kessler
1977	Sharon Rappaport, Martin Rappaport
6-25-1978	Gillian Gemmell, Even Dreslinger
1978	Judith McCartney, Steven Levy
1978	Cindy Stein, Ben Finkel
1979	Mitzi Levy, Adam Levy
1981	Ilene Saltz, Max Clark
1982	Leslie Sussan, Richard Groden
1982	Kathy Nacosky, Ben Schneider
1982	Marcee Gaman, Daniel Lundeen

1982	Melissa Sommer, Kevin Katz
1982	Linda Manheimer, Robert Cuneo
1983	Janine Crown, Joseph Steagall
1983	Susan Lipnick, Robert Lynch
1986	Kim Smith, Andrew Mytelka
9-1-1990	Marshall and Lydia Stein
1990	Ann Anderson, Tom Kent
1991	Darryl and Syma Levy
3-3-1991	Bill Rosenberg
1991	Natalie Joel Ginsberg, Sam Bazaman
1991	Mandy Gilbert, David Nathan
1991	Corey Rubin, Rabbi Ted Reiter
1991	Cynthia Brown, Steven Nussenblatt
1992	Tal Simmons, Jon Spiegel
1992	Lisa Bryant, Steven Levy
1992	Kay Weinstock, Robert Rose
1992	Cathey Pomeroy, Steven Blackwell
1992	Linda MacDonald, John Fernandez
1990	Deborah Warren, Bruce Steckler
1993	Sandy Stein, Brent Richbook
1996	Helen Swiff, Jason Goodman
1997	Ellen More, Micha Hofri
1998	Ari Rose, Niels Ries
1999	Sandra Beasly, David Schwarz
1999	Michael Goldberg, Louise Fishman
2000	Pamela Clanton, Mitchell Wilson
2001	Naomi Shabot, Brian Wittlin
2002	Daniel Maslin, Sarah Shabot
5-31-2003	Todd and Meredith Masel
8-16-2003	Marsha Wilson, Mitchell Rappaport

CULTURE IN ACTION

Hip-Hop

Jim Mack

Raintree

Chicago, Illinois

www.heinemannraintree.com

Visit our website to find out more information about Heinemann-Raintree books.

To order:

☎ Phone 888-454-2279

💻 Visit www.heinemannraintree.com to browse our catalog and order online.

Edited by Louise Galpine, Abby Colich, and Laura J. Hensley
Designed by Kimberly Miracle and Betsy Wernert
Original illustrations © Capstone Global Library Ltd.
Illustrated by kja-artists.com
Picture research by Hannah Taylor
Production by Alison Parsons
Originated by Dot Gradations Ltd.
Printed and Bound in the United States
by Corporate Graphics

13 12 11 10 09
10 9 8 7 6 5 4 3 2 1

Library of Congress Cataloging-in-Publication Data

Mack, Jim.
  Hip-hop / Jim Mack.
       p. cm. -- (Culture in action)
  Includes bibliographical references and index.
  ISBN 978-1-4109-3393-5 (hc) -- ISBN 978-1-4109-3410-9 (pb)
  1. Hip-hop dance--Juvenile literature. I. Title.
  GV1796.H57M33 2008
  793.3--dc22
                              2008053046

Acknowledgments

The author and publishers are grateful to the following for permission to reproduce copyright material: Corbis pp. **6** (Thinkstock), **8** (Brenda Ann Kenneally), **19 right** (Neal Preston), **22** (James Leynse), **25** (Reuters/Ethan Miller), **26** (epa/Joelle Diderich); Getty Images pp. **4** (Stone/Bruno De Hogues), **5** (Ty Milford), **7** (Antonio Luiz Hamdan), **10** (WireImage/Jemal Countess), **14** (Jason Blaney), **17** (FilmMagic/Lyle A. Waisman), **18 bottom** (Rick Diamond), **19 left** (Peter Kramer), **20 bottom** (WireImage/Kevin Mazur), **21 top** (WireImage/Arnold Turner), **21 bottom** (WireImage/Bob Levey), **24** (Vince Bucci); Photolibrary p. **12** (Tony Hopewell); Redferns pp. **11** (Janette Beckman), **13** (Ebet Roberts); Rex Features pp. **18 top** (Leon Schadeberg), **20 top** (Geoff Robinson), **27** (Voisin/Phanie). Shutterstock p. **16** (© charobnica).

Icon and banner images supplied by Shutterstock: © Alexander Lukin, © ornitopter, © Colorlife, and © David S. Rose.

Cover photograph of a DJ playing music reproduced with permission of Corbis/Blend Images/Andersen Ross.

We would like to thank Nancy Harris and Jackie Murphy for their invaluable help in the preparation of this book.

Every effort has been made to contact copyright holders of any material reproduced in this book. Any omissions will be rectified in subsequent printings if notice is given to the publisher.

All the Internet addresses (URLs) given in this book were valid at the time of going to press. However, due to the dynamic nature of the Internet, some addresses may have changed, or sites may have changed or ceased to exist since publication. While the author and publisher regret any inconvenience this may cause readers, no responsibility for any such changes can be accepted by either the author or the publisher.

Contents

Some words are printed in bold, **like this**. You can find out what they mean by looking in the glossary on page 30.

Planet Hip-Hop

In a club, an **MC raps** into a microphone while a **DJ mixes** records. The work of **graffiti** artists decorates a wall outside, and teenagers are **break-dancing** on the sidewalk. Hip-hop is not just a musical style. It is a **culture** (way of life) that started on the streets of New York City in the 1970s. It quickly spread throughout the United States and the rest of the world.

Hip-hop is rooted in the **rhythms** (regular beats) of African and Caribbean music. It mixes rhythmic, repetitive song with rhymed storytelling. Hip-hop musicians combine styles of music such as rock, jazz, soul, rhythm and blues (R&B), and more.

Music through the decades

The **lyrics** (words) of rock and folk music in the 1960s often centered on problems in the changing world. Music in the 1970s was generally less serious. This included the lighthearted dance music of disco. Hip-hop exploded in the mid-1980s. It had a completely different sound than anything that had come before it.

Drums are an important part of traditional African music.

Art and self-expression are what hip-hop culture is all about.

Parts of hip-hop

Hip-hop culture consists of four major parts: the DJ, the MC, graffiti, and break-dancing. Each part of hip-hop is an art form. All types of hip-hop artist are constantly trying to be the best. This is good for hip-hop. It means that the artists are always inventing new styles. This book mostly focuses on the music side of hip-hop—the DJs and MCs.

What Is Hip-Hop?

There are many things that go into making a hip-hop song. It starts with energetic music played by a **DJ**, or disc jockey. The DJ usually plays two vinyl records at the same time. He or she spins these records on two **turntables** (record players). The turntables are connected to a mixer. This allows the DJ to **mix** records. Mixing means the DJ slides a switch back and forth to play music from each turntable on its own, or both at the same time. Modern DJs also use computers, drum machines (electronic devices that sound like drums), **synthesizers** (keyboard-like instruments), and other devices to create music.

The **MC**, or master of ceremonies, **raps** over the beat of the music. To rap is to make rhymes with words, like reciting a poem. An MC often has a gift for using words, creating thoughtful **lyrics** and clever rhymes.

Rap or hip-hop?

The words *rap* and *hip-hop* are often thought to mean the same thing. Rap refers to lyrics said or rapped by an MC. Hip-hop refers to the **culture** as a whole. Rap is a part of hip-hop culture.

An MC and DJ work together to create hip-hop music.

Learning to be a DJ requires a lot of practice.
It is like learning to play an instrument.

Other players

A band also can be used to create hip-hop
music. The Roots are a hip-hop band. They
use instruments to make music that sounds
like a hip-hop DJ.

Some hip-hop artists are **beat-boxers**.
Beat-boxers use their tongues, mouths,
lips, and voices to create a beat. U.S. rapper
Doug E. Fresh never even had a DJ or band.
He did everything with his mouth.
Biz Markie was also well known for his
beat-boxing abilities.

Multiple MCs

Many hip-hop groups have more than
one MC. Some of these groups include:
Grandmaster Flash and the Furious Five
Wu-Tang Clan
Jurassic 5
Run-DMC
Beastie Boys
De La Soul
A Tribe Called Quest

Write and sing your own rap

Creating hip-hop music involves hard work and practice. Listening, writing, and reading are important skills in rapping. They are part of the creative process that goes into rapping.

Steps to follow:

1. Listen to a few hip-hop songs for ideas. Try "Rapper's Delight" by the Sugarhill Gang. Hip-hop artists often listen to other music and musicians to find their own ideas. Pay attention to how the MCs rhyme. They might rap smoothly or in a choppy way.

2. Pick six words that rhyme.

3. Put each word in a sentence so that it is like a story. Use a dictionary, thesaurus, or rhyming dictionary if you need help.

4. Rap your new lyrics to a hip-hop song or create a new beat for your rap. Have a friend try to beat-box by making noises with his or her mouth as you rap. You can both tap your feet or clap your hands.

Spending time experimenting with and learning new words is how hip-hop artists (like Yykkes, shown here) become great.

Tools of the trade

You can use a dictionary to look up words you do not know. Also try using a thesaurus. It will give you lists of words that mean the same or the opposite of a particular word. A rhyming dictionary will give you lists of rhyming words.

While writing a hip-hop song, an MC will often try rapping the lyrics out loud to see if they sound good.

5. Rap your lyrics out loud to yourself or your friends.

6. Repeat the process to create several short raps or a whole song.

Example

I'm real fast, and here I come.

My words are quick and so fun.

I won't quit, until I'm done.

You can't catch me, when I run.

I just can't stop, and like the sun,

I'll shine my rhymes on everyone!

History in the Making

Hip-hop began in the early 1970s in poor African-American and Afro-Caribbean neighborhoods in New York City. **DJs** would play at gatherings and parties held in the streets and public parks. They would plug a sound system into a streetlight's power source to play music.

Hey, DJ—Play that song!

Hip-hop first received attention in 1973. At that time, Jamaican-born DJ Kool Herc stood out among other DJs. He started to extend the "break" of songs. This is the part of a song that occurs somewhere between the middle and end. At this point there is no singing and a drumbeat takes over. Herc extended the break of songs by using two copies of the same record and cutting back and forth, creating what is known as a **break beat**.

DJ Kool Herc began his career DJing at block parties and in parks.

By the mid- to late 1970s, people started to notice other DJs who used Herc's style. One was Afrika Bambaataa, who led a tough street gang. In time, Bambaataa would convert his gang into the Zulu Nation. This is a group dedicated to peace, unity, harmony, and hip-hop. The Zulu Nation helped to bring hip-hop to Europe.

Grandmaster Flash would become more popular than Herc because of his skill and speed at spinning records (see box below right). Grandmaster Flash and his group, the Furious Five, led the way in **MCing** and **freestyle rapping** competitions (see box below).

Afrika Bambaataa became known as the "Master of Records." This was because of his huge collection of records.

Competitive hip-hop

Some MCs compete in freestyle and battle raps on stage, or even on the street, to verbally prove who is more skilled. Freestyle rapping is rapping without preparing first. Battle rapping is attacking another MC with freestyle bragging and boasting raps.

"Who's spinning tonight?"

DJs spin records on **turntables**. So, "spinning" is another name for DJing.

Beyond the streets

In 1979 hip-hop went **mainstream**, meaning many people became aware of it. The song "Rapper's Delight" is thought to be the first song that popularized hip-hop. It was by a little-known group called the Sugarhill Gang from Englewood, New Jersey. Early DJs such as Herc, Bambaataa, and Flash had once been upset that their music was not being played on the radio. Now hip-hop had finally managed to announce itself to the world.

Sampling music

Sampling is when DJs or **producers** (people who direct the recording process) use a turntable, computer, or tape player to extract (pull out or copy) part of a song. They might extract a catchy beat or break. This part of the song is then taken, or sampled, and used in a new song.

Record hunting

DJs are highly competitive. In order to be different and have the best music, they spend a lot of time looking for uncommon records and sounds. DJs also look for two copies of the same record in order to create the break beat.

A DJ will visit many different record stores, resale shops, and even yard sales looking for records to try.

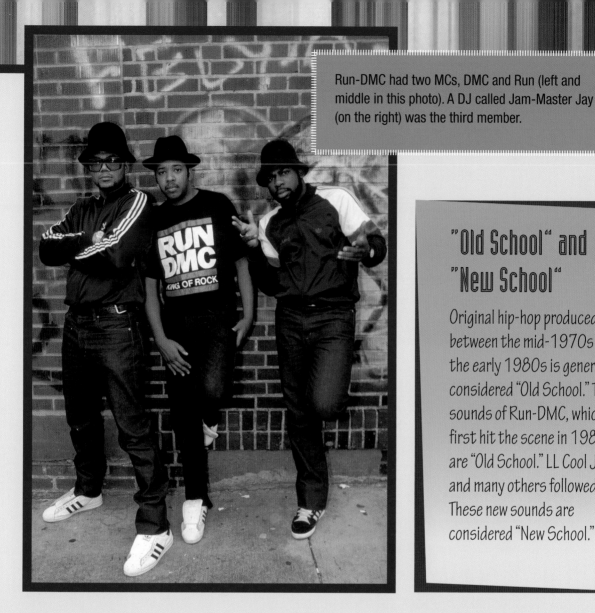

Run-DMC had two MCs, DMC and Run (left and middle in this photo). A DJ called Jam-Master Jay (on the right) was the third member.

"Old School" and "New School"

Original hip-hop produced between the mid-1970s to the early 1980s is generally considered "Old School." The sounds of Run-DMC, which first hit the scene in 1983, are "Old School." LL Cool J and many others followed. These new sounds are considered "New School."

The group Run-DMC became popular in 1983. Their sound featured rapping with rhyming **lyrics**. It had little backing music other than heavy drumbeats. Until that time, hip-hop audiences had mostly heard a dance beat.

The Beastie Boys are a three-man group from New York City. In 1986 they became the first popular white hip-hop act in the United States. Their youthful and clever rapping style made them a popular mainstream group. They helped to make hip-hop familiar to white audiences.

Music is a major part of hip-hop **culture**. But from its early history, art forms such as **break-dancing** and **graffiti** have also made important contributions to hip-hop.

Break-dancing

During the early days of hip-hop, dancers who would dance during the "break" of a song became known as break boys or break girls, or "b-boys" and "b-girls." In 1977 a famous group of breakers, the Rock Steady Crew, formed. They helped make the dancing style popular. Today, break boys and break girls dance at competitions, parties, or even on the streets.

Graffiti

The first graffiti art was big, colorful, and competitive. In this way, it was just like other parts of hip-hop culture. Graffiti artists used highlighted outlines and wild designs. But graffiti that is spray-painted on walls of people's property is an act of **vandalism**. It is illegal. Some graffiti artists went from making illegal artwork to having their art shown in galleries.

Create a basic hip-hop dance

Break-dancing is an **improvisational** way to dance. This means you have to be able to perform without preparing ahead of time. "Top rocking" is moving the arms while the body remains in an upright position. Using the ground to complete moves such as spins, flips, and other leg movements is called "floor rocking." Try creating your own hip-hop dance.

Steps to follow:

1. Start with your feet together.

2. Slide your right foot away from your left foot.

3. Slide your left foot back next to your right.

4. Clap your hands.

5. Repeat the process going the opposite way.

6. Add the movement of nodding your head up and down.

7. Don't be afraid to try some dance moves, too. Try spinning around in a circle on your feet or your back.

8. Practice your new dance routine.

9. Turn on a hip-hop song and perform your dance for others.

Hip-hop is about creativity. People can make up their own new dance moves and blend them together with old ones.

Hip-Hop Artists

Hip-hop artists and styles in the United States today are classified, or sorted, into territories: the East Coast, West Coast, Midwest, and South.

Hip-hop territories

East Coast hip-hop music is typically known for its well-spoken **lyrics** about **urban** (city) life. It is also known for irregular, powerful beats.

West Coast hip-hop became known for "gangsta **rap**." This style of hip-hop uses slow, intense rhymes about gangs and violence. It uses smooth, regular beats.

The style of Midwestern hip-hop has been heavily influenced by all forms of hip-hop. There is nothing typical about Midwestern hip-hop. Few hip-hop artists from the Midwest share the same sound.

The music of Southern hip-hop, also known as "Dirty South," has an upbeat style that uses mostly simple and fun lyrics.

Different parts of the United States have unique styles of hip-hop.

Styles of hip-hop

Artists today create many types of hip-hop music. One type is about learning, problems in the world, and sometimes religion. Common, A Tribe Called Quest, De La Soul, and Mos Def are a few hip-hop artists who make this style of music.

Other artists create a type of hip-hop that is concerned with government. It also encourages listeners to explore different ideas and thoughts. Public Enemy was one of the first well-known hip-hop groups to use this style.

Mainstream and underground

Mainstream is music that receives a lot of attention from media such as newspapers, magazines, and television. It is often created to sell albums and make money. **Underground** hip-hop artists are those outside the mainstream. The lyrics of underground artists are often more respected than those of the mainstream. They usually focus on more mature and thoughtful topics. Some underground hip-hop groups move into the mainstream. Two popular underground artists are MF Doom and Cool Kids.

Cool Kids are a popular underground group from the Midwest.

Hip-hop stars

Many different artists have come out of the four hip-hop territories in the United States. The next few pages highlight just a small number of them.

East Coast

Jay-Z is from Brooklyn, New York. He became a street **hustler** when he was a child, getting involved in questionable activities. Later he created his own record label, named Roc-A-Fella Records, to start his own hip-hop career. His first album, *Reasonable Doubt*, was released in 1996. In 2004 Jay-Z became president of Def Jam Records. He is one of the most successful hip-hop artists ever.

Nas is from Queens, New York. As a young man he read many books and wrote short stories and poetry. His **gritty** (tough) and intelligent rhymes brought him fame and success. His first album, *Illmatic*, was released in 1994. It is in the East Coast style.

Jay-Z helped start a clothing company called Rocawear.

Nas began as an underground rapper in New York City.

Lauryn Hill is one of the most respected female hip-hop artists.

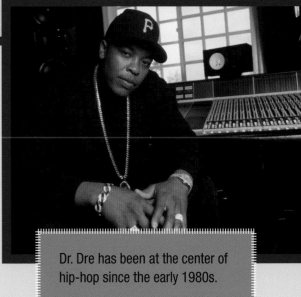

Dr. Dre has been at the center of hip-hop since the early 1980s.

Lauryn Hill is from South Orange, New Jersey. As a teenager, Hill sang on the television program *Showtime at the Apollo*. She also had a role on the soap opera *As the World Turns*. In high school she formed the band the Fugees with two of her friends. Their second album, *The Score*, released in 1996, won many awards. Her solo album *Miseducation of Lauryn Hill*, released in 1998, was a global success.

West Coast

Dr. Dre is from Los Angeles, California. He played a part in the creation of the "gangsta rap" style. Dr. Dre helped form Death Row Records in 1991. He combined booming beats along with **funk** music to create the "G-Funk" style. Funk is bass-heavy music characterized by **improvisation** (performing without preparing), horns, and strong **rhythms**. He is a successful music **producer** and has helped to create hits for artists such as Snoop Dogg, 50 Cent, Eve, the Game, and Young Buck.

West Coast underground

The following are some important West Coast underground artists:
Freestyle Fellowship
Pharcyde
Souls of Mischief
Hieroglyphics
Dilated Peoples
People Under the Stairs

Midwest

Kanye West is from Chicago, Illinois. He left college to pursue a hip-hop career. He began producing songs for Chicago artists. Later, he produced music for Nas and Jay-Z. West released his first album, *The College Dropout*, in 2004. He has had great success creating his own new music and producing for others.

Kanye West is known for his bold fashion choices and attitude.

Eminem was born in Kansas City, Missouri, but lived in Detroit, Michigan, as a teenager. In 1997 he took second place in a **freestyle** battle rap contest (see page 11) in Los Angeles, California. Dr. Dre took notice and added Eminem to his record label. Eminem became a popular underground rapper. After his *Slim Shady* album was released in 1999, he became one of the best-selling rappers of all time.

Eminem starred in a movie based on his life called *8 Mile*.

André 3000 and Big Boi have also pursued acting careers.

South

OutKast are from Atlanta, Georgia. André 3000 and Big Boi went to high school together and were rival rappers until 1992, when the two formed OutKast. They released *Southernplayalisticadillacmuzik* in 1994. Their clever lyrics and smooth songs helped to define the Southern hip-hop style.

Lil Wayne is from New Orleans, Louisiana. He joined the rap group Hot Boys when he was a teenager. He helped form the record label Cash Money Records. From 2003 until 2008, he became famous by releasing **mixtapes**. These are CDs of an artist's music that are given out for free to attract fans. Lil Wayne has gone on to record music with many artists. He has worked on over 100 different music projects!

Lil Wayne has a unique-sounding voice and wild lyrics.

The Business

Successful hip-hop artists make a lot of money recording music. Record companies and other industries have also realized they can make money from hip-hop. Some hip-hop artists have started their own record companies. Others have created fashion, film, and television careers linked to hip-hop.

The record business

The first hip-hop artists created a new sound and style because they loved the music. In time, hip-hop artists began to make money from their music. Making money by doing something they loved became a dream for many hip-hop artists. When an artist signs a record deal, he or she can make a lot of money.

Getting signed

Becoming "signed" to a record label is a long process. First, you have to be able to make music that people like. Musicians often practice for many years before even playing in front of an audience. They make recordings to give to record labels. The record labels listen to their music before deciding whether or not to help them make a record.

Def Jam

Russell Simmons and Rick Rubin started the first major hip-hop record label while they were at New York University. Def Jam would go on to launch the careers of Run-DMC, the Beastie Boys, LL Cool J, Public Enemy, and many other hip-hop artists.

Russell Simmons is a leading figure in the business of hip-hop.

Make a hip-hop poster

Record companies create posters to tell fans about hip-hop music and concerts. Use words, pictures, drawings, and color to create a poster of your favorite hip-hop artist. You could also create one for your own hip-hop group.

Steps to follow:

1. Decide what your poster will tell others about: a group, a new album, or a concert?

2. Picture in your head what you want the poster to look like. What words will it use? What pictures will you use?

3. Use solid colors to draw pictures and use big, bubbly words (see the sample poster at right).

4. Use a dark color to outline all the words and pictures.

5. Use other colors to add detail to the poster.

6. Display your poster for others to see.

As you make your poster, listen to the music and let it inspire you to create something great.

Beats, Boasts, and Beyond

The world of hip-hop is constantly changing. In the early 21st century, many hip-hop artists focused on glamour and wealth. Sean Combs, also known as "Puff Daddy," "P-Diddy," and "Diddy," played a major role in glamorizing hip-hop with flashy songs. He **sampled** catchy music in party songs. He **rapped** about the "bling-bling" style of expensive things such as jewelry and cars.

Recent trends

The trends among other hip-hop artists in recent years vary widely. Some artists are positive and others are not. Hip-hop artists rap about many things. Some rap about what concerns them. They also tell stories. Some rappers are funny. Some try to teach important life lessons. Others are serious. Some use **profanity** (offensive words).

Sean Combs started a successful label called Bad Boy Records.

Choose wisely

Your parents, caregivers, or teachers should know what music you are listening to. They will tell you if what you are listening to is okay.

A hip-hop concert, such as this Pharrell Williams event, is exciting for fans. It is also an opportunity for an artist to spread important messages to fans, such as nonviolence.

Hip-hop anniversary tour

In 2008 several hip-hop artists got together for the No Profanity Hip-Hop Anniversary Tour. Several hip-hop artists performed at different locations throughout the United States and Europe. Some of the artists who performed were Grandmaster Mele Mel, Big Daddy Kane, Afrika Bambaataa and the SoulSonic Force, and Public Enemy. The artists used the tour to tell people about No Profanity Day (August 9, 2009). Their goal was for there to be no crime, violence, hate, or profanity on that day.

The beat goes on

Hip-hop music started small. From poor neighborhoods in New York City, it quickly spread all over the world. Today, major hip-hop acts are emerging from Europe. In the United Kingdom, the Streets and Dizzee Rascal (see box below) are known for their clever rhymes, while female rapper M.I.A. has political messages. In other parts of Europe, **MCs** like Bligg and Stress rap in languages other than English, including German and French.

Dizzee Rascal

Dizzee Rascal was born in London, England, and has become a successful rapper and record **producer**. In 2003, at age 18, he was the youngest person ever to win the Mercury Prize for his album *Boy in da Corner*. The Mercury Prize is a yearly prize given for the best album in the United Kingdom. He raps using a "grime" style that is unique to MCs from the United Kingdom. Grime is similar to U.S. hip-hop, but it uses faster electronic beats and even faster rhymes.

Dizzee Rascal is a popular British hip-hop artist.

As long as there is an audience for hip-hop, new stars and new styles will continue to emerge.

The future of hip-hop

Hip-hop sales have fallen by more than 40 percent since the year 2000. Illegal copying is one reason why sales have gone down. Illegal copying is when people use a computer to copy songs and share them without paying for them. Another reason is that since 2000, audiences have become bored with the focus on violence and wealth in hip-hop.

Although hip-hop record sales have fallen over the last few years, many new hip-hop artists still record music every day. New artists are played on the radio all the time. Hip-hop will continue to develop and change with new messages and exciting new styles of music.

Timeline

1970s	New York **DJs** Afrika Bambaataa and Grandmaster Flash begin their careers. They will become stars by the early 1980s.
1973	DJ Kool Herc begins DJing parties and develops the **break beat**. This inspires **break-dancing**.
1977	The famous group of break-dancers, the Rock Steady Crew, is formed.
1979	The Sugarhill Gang releases the hip-hop hit "Rapper's Delight."
	Grandmaster Flash joins with the **MCs** known as the Furious Five.
1981	The Zulu Nation begins spreading hip-hop to Europe.
1983	Run-DMC brings MCing to the forefront of hip-hop.
1984	Rick Rubin and Russell Simmons start the hip-hop record label Def Jam.
1986	The Beastie Boys release the album *Licensed to Ill*, to **mainstream** success.
1988	Public Enemy releases the political album *It Takes a Nation of Millions to Hold Us Back*.
	N.W.A. popularizes gangsta **rap** with its first album, *Straight Outta Compton*.
1992	Death Row Records is formed and releases Dr. Dre's gangsta rap album *The Chronic*.
1994	Common releases the politically conscious hip-hop album *Resurrection*.

1996	The Fugees release the popular album *The Score*.
	Jay-Z starts Roc-A-Fella Records and releases his first album, *Reasonable Doubt*.
1998	Lauryn Hill releases *The Miseducation of Lauryn Hill*.
1999	Dr. Dre releases *2001* and is the **producer** of Eminem's first album, *The Slim Shady LP*.
	Hip-hop becomes the top-selling type of music in the United States, with 81 million albums sold.
2000	Hip-hop album sales begin to drop.
2003	Lil Wayne begins releasing **mixtapes**.
	50 Cent's *Get Rich or Die Tryin'* is released.
2006	Nas is signed with Def Jam and releases the album *Hip-Hop Is Dead*.
2008	**Underground** hip-hop artists like Lupe Fiasco, B.o.B, Kidz in the Hall, Kid Sister, and Cool Kids begin to emerge.
2009	Legendary hip-hop stars such as Dr. Dre, Eminem, 50 Cent, Jay-Z, and the Beastie Boys release albums. So do newer artists such as Kid Sister and Lupe Fiasco.

Glossary

beat-boxing using the lips, mouth, tongue, and hands to sound like drums and other musical sounds

break beat extended drumbeat in a hip-hop song

break-dancing form of hip-hop dance that uses the hands and feet for exciting spin and flip movements, both standing and on the ground

culture way of life for a certain group of people

DJ short for "disc jockey," a person who plays recorded music

freestyle rapping on the spot without preparing, by using any rhymes that come to mind

funk bass-heavy musical style characterized by improvisation, horns, and strong rhythms

graffiti markings or drawings often found on buildings and sidewalks, usually made with spray paint

gritty displaying a hard and tough style

hustler someone who makes money through illegal or questionable ways, such as selling drugs or stealing

improvisational performing without preparing

lyrics words to a song

mainstream music that receives a lot of attention from newspapers, magazines, and television

MC short for "master of ceremonies"

mix play two records at the same time or each on their own using a switch that connects two turntables

mixtape collection of songs and freestyles usually recorded by a hip-hop artist on a CD. This CD is released on the Internet or handed out for free on the street or at a concert to promote the new hip-hop artist.

producer someone who directs the recording process and also creates music

profanity words or actions that are offensive

rap lyrics said to a rhythm, often as rhymes, by an MC in a hip-hop song. Also, the act of saying these lyrics.

rhythm in music, a rhythm is a regular beat

sample use a turntable, computer, or tape player to copy part of a song, such as a catchy beat or break

synthesizer instrument that usually resembles a keyboard and makes complex, interesting sounds

turntable record player. It uses a needle that glides across the record to make a sound.

underground music that has not become popular on television or radio, but still has many fans

urban found in or characteristic of living in a city

vandalism purposely destroying property

Find Out More

Books

Fitzgerald, Tamsin. *Hip-Hop and Urban Dance* (*Dance*). Chicago: Heinemann Library, 2009.

Giovanni, Nikki. *Hip Hop Speaks to Children: A Celebration of Poetry with a Beat*. Naperville, Ill.: Sourcebooks Jabberwocky, 2008.

Waters, Rosa. *Hip-Hop: A Short History*. Broomall, Pa.: Mason Crest, 2007.

Websites

A list of hip-hop music for kids (click on "hip-hop" from the list on the left)
www.commonsensemedia.org/music-reviews

KidzWorld's "Pioneers of Hip Hop"
www.kidzworld.com/article/5321-pioneers-of-hip-hop

Index